NEW DIRECTIONS FOR HIGHER EDUCATION

Martin Kramer
EDITOR-IN-CHIEF

Developing and Implementing Service-Learning Programs

Mark Canada, Bruce W. Speck
University of North Carolina at Pembroke

EDITORS

Number 114, Summer 2001

JOSSEY-BASS
San Francisco

DEVELOPING AND IMPLEMENTING SERVICE-LEARNING PROGRAMS
Mark Canada, Bruce W. Speck (eds.)
New Directions for Higher Education, no. 114
Martin Kramer, Editor-in-Chief

Microfilm copies of issues and articles are available in 16mm and 35mm, as well as microfiche in 105mm, through University Microfilms Inc., 300 North Zeeb Road, Ann Arbor, Michigan 48106-1346.

ISSN 0271-0560   ISBN 0-7879-5782-8

NEW DIRECTIONS FOR HIGHER EDUCATION is part of The Jossey-Bass Higher and Adult Education Series and is published quarterly by Jossey-Bass Inc., 350 Sansome Street, San Francisco, California 94104-1342. Periodicals postage paid at San Francisco, California, and at additional mailing offices. Postmaster: Send address changes to New Directions for Higher Education, Jossey-Bass Inc., 350 Sansome Street, San Francisco, California 94104-1342.

SUBSCRIPTIONS cost $59 for individuals and $114 for institutions, agencies, and libraries. See Ordering Information page at end of book.

EDITORIAL CORRESPONDENCE should be sent to the Editor-in-Chief, Martin Kramer, 2807 Shasta Road, Berkeley, California 94708-2011.

Cover photograph and random dot by Richard Blair/Color & Light © 1990.

Jossey-Bass Web address: www.josseybass.com

CONTENTS

Editors' Notes

Service-learning is the coupling of academic work that students do in a classroom with students' service to an organization outside the classroom. The academic work and the service are completed together, so that students both study issues and become participants in the outworking of those issues in a particular community setting. In this way, students learn through the integration of theory and practice.

The primary goal of service-learning is to foster responsible citizenship and, consequently, to promote students' lifelong involvement in helping to solve social issues. This goal is flavored by the particular theoretical base a professor chooses to inform his or her understanding of service-learning, but the most inclusive goal of service-learning is fostering long-term citizenship that is willing to roll up its sleeves and promote a better life for those who suffer "the slings and arrows of outrageous fortune."

This volume looks at how service-learning can be implemented in the classroom by providing viewpoints on implementing service-learning in particular academic contexts. The first seven chapters address broad theoretical and practical matters of interest to both faculty new to the field and veterans looking for ways to improve their service-learning.

Chapter One, by Bruce W. Speck, sets the stage for understanding service-learning by explaining two significant theoretical approaches to service-learning (philanthropic and civil) so that professors are aware of two different impulses that inform service-learning. In addition, it addresses three critical concerns about service-learning.

Chapter Two, by Maureen Shubow Rubin, sets out a seven-step development model that professors new to service-learning can use to prepare and conduct a service-learning course.

In Chapter Three, Robert Shumer explains how professors can engage disabled students in service-learning, noting that such students are good candidates for providing service to others.

Janet Eyler gives detailed advice in Chapter Four on how professors can use reflection in their service-learning courses. Reflection is a critical component because it allows students to respond, often in writing, to the relationship between what they are learning in class and what they are experiencing in their service site.

Chapter Five, by Mark Canada, makes the point that computer technology is a prime way to enable students to serve their communities, particularly when students help agencies create and update Web sites.

Chapter Six, by Barbara A. Holland, deals with the increasingly important issue of assessment. It discusses a comprehensive model for evaluating the impact of service-learning on students and on the organizations students serve.

In Chapter Seven, Lawrence Neil Bailis examines the ways that national organizations, particularly the National Society for Experiential Education, can help faculty improve service-learning.

The next three chapters explore the possibilities and challenges of using service-learning in various academic contexts. In Chapter Eight, Andrew Furco notes the difficulties of promoting service-learning at research universities and provides ideas about how to overcome those challenges. Chapter Nine, by Kathy O'Byrne, shows how service-learning can be promoted at teaching institutions, which are natural sites for integrating the rigors of academic scholarship and learning through service. And Chapter Ten, by Edward Zlotkowski, provides a cogent argument for the necessity of service-learning at liberal arts colleges, institutions in some ways ideally suited for this brand of education.

Finally, in Chapter Eleven, Elaine K. Ikeda lists and explains the value of particular resources that professors may consult to broaden their academic kit of service-learning tools.

As several authors point out, service-learning is a relatively new pedagogy, so professors who are new to it will want concrete information about how to develop and sustain a service-learning course. This book provides advice, information, and models that they can use to form a union between theory and practice that will enrich students' learning and prepare them to engage in service to their communities throughout their lives.

Mark Canada
Bruce W. Speck
Editors

MARK CANADA teaches English at the University of North Carolina at Pembroke and edits the educational Internet site "All American: Literature, History, and Culture" (www.uncp.edu/home/canada/work/allam/allam.htm).

BRUCE W. SPECK is dean of the College of Arts and Sciences at the University of North Carolina at Pembroke.

1

*Before engaging in service-learning, professors will
want to know what the impulses are behind service-
learning, what research says about the successes
and pitfalls of service-learning, and how they can
respond to major objections to it.*

Why Service-Learning?

Bruce W. Speck

To ask the question, Why service-learning? in a volume designed to provide
professors with the nuts and bolts of implementing service-learning in their
classes might appear a bit odd. After all, does service-learning need any
rationale? Isn't it a bit of common sense that the study of academic subjects
is linked in tangible ways to life outside the classroom? Isn't it transparently
obvious that learning cannot be adequately defined by the mere amassing
of knowledge—of facts, figures, and theories so readily available in higher
education classrooms?

The answer to those supposedly rhetorical questions is not a resound-
ing yes. In fact, service-learning needs a great deal of explanation. First,
there is no one impulse behind service-learning initiatives, and professors
should understand the reasoning behind the various impulses. Although
this chapter is not designed to provide a detailed explanation of theoretical assumptions that support service-learning, nevertheless, professors,
who are acutely aware of the theoretical underpinnings for practical
endeavors, will be curious about the assumptions that support service-
learning. Second, professors, quite reasonably, will want to know to what
extent service-learning initiatives have been successful. Indeed, studies can
provide insight into service-learning approaches that have shown success
in meeting particular service-learning goals and those that have shown
potential pitfalls in meeting those goals. Third, professors certainly will
want to know the answers to major objections regarding service-learning.
It would be naive to assume that professors, chief proponents of critical
thinking, would not be interested in reasoned responses to objections
brought against service-learning or would make a decision to engage in
service-learning without exploring answers to potential problems. My task,

therefore, is to provide information about all three of these issues so that professors have an informed framework for making decisions about engaging in service-learning.

Impulses for Service-Learning

To discuss the impulses that support service-learning, I begin with three definitions:

> In their most limited sense, service learning courses unite in a single mission the traditionally separate duties of research, teaching, and service. [Cushman, 1999, p. 331]

> More than volunteerism, service-learning combines community work with classroom instruction, emphasizing reflection as well as action. It empowers students by making them responsible in a real world context, while giving them the support, encouragement, information, and skills to be effective. [Rosenberg, 2000, p. 8]

> Service learning is a pedagogy that fosters the development of skills and knowledge needed for participation in public life. [Forman and Wilkinson, 1997, p. 278]

These definitions have common threads: (1) separation and (2) integration and engagement.

Concerning separation, Cushman (1999) says that the mission of higher education comprises three duties that are not interrelated: research, teaching, and service. Rosenberg (2000) assumes that students are not being empowered in the traditional classroom; rather, they are actually separated from the means of empowerment. The problem of empowerment appears to be related to the separation of an "unreal" world of education from a real-world context. Forman and Wilkinson (1997) also suggest that traditional education separates students from participation in public life and in fact does not give them the skills and knowledge they need for such participation. In all three cases, service-learning is a way to overcome separation by integration and engagement. Concerning integration and engagement, service-learning unites research, teaching, and service; combines community work with classroom instruction; and prepares students to participate in public life, thus integrating theory and practice.

These definitions faithfully represent a main intention of service-learning: to ensure that academic study is integrated with the larger public life, generally conceived as life outside the classroom, although the classroom is a place where students also develop community relationships. The definitions also represent a negative critique of traditional education as ineffective in fostering the skills and attitudes necessary for students to become active in solving social problems.

The definitions, however, do not reveal two motives for service-learning, which Battistoni (1997) defines as "philanthropic and civic" (p. 150), which provide two very different impulses for service-learning. The philanthropic position might also be considered an additive position. It holds that all that needs to be done to the traditional classroom is to add a public service component. Public service is integrated into the classroom by ensuring that students consider the impact of service, but the impulse behind the philanthropic or additive approach is helping others who are in need of help, with the added benefit of honing students' marketable skills and encouraging students to feel good about themselves.

The civic approach is at odds with the philanthropic or additive approach and constitutes a radical pedagogy. It assumes that (1) the American social order is fragmented, lacking a sense of community, (2) lack of community has produced injustices of various kinds, (3) higher education is deeply implicated in the perpetuation of injustice, and (4) higher education must be radically transformed to meet its obligation to produce citizens who can promote justice in a democratic society.

The philanthropic-additive approach and the civic approach are very different approaches to service-learning, and professors should investigate each to make an informed decision about their philosophical commitment to service-learning. In investigating the two basic impulses, they will find in the service-learning literature degrees of commitment along a continuum, with the philanthropic-additive approach near one end of the continuum and the civic approach near the other end. In fact, the literature offers both models (Cleary, 1998; Cleary and Benson, 1998; Gordon, 1999; Schaeffer and Peterson, 1998) and examples of classroom service-learning (Althaus, 1997; Bush-Bacelis, 1998; Eddy and Carducci, 1997; Huckin, 1997; Mohan, 1995; Ogburn and Wallace, 1998) at different points along the continuum. My purpose is to provide a discussion of the civic approach because it appears to represent a highly powerful impulse in the developing pedagogy of service-learning, and I assume that professors will want to know more about a pedagogy that both threatens the status quo of higher education and promises remarkable benefits once the status quo is replaced by the structures necessary to sustain a long-term service-learning pedagogy.

Service-learning is not new in terms of its intellectual roots, which as Morton and Saltmarsh (1997) show, go back to the Progressive era in U.S. history, particularly the work of Jane Addams, John Dewey, and Dorothy Day. At the same time, as Barber and Battistoni (1993) note, it "is [in] some ways a rather new pedagogy" (p. ix). Its newness is quite obvious when its literature is investigated. I did a search of the word *service-learning* using the ERIC database and found six sources in 1990, five in 1991, two in 1992, and then sixty in 1996, fifty-two in 1997, fifty-three in 1998, and forty-six in 1999. Clearly, *service-learning* as a searchable term is relatively new, and the literature about it has increased significantly in the past five or six years.

Another way that it is new is that it is a response to a perceived fragmentation of community and the ascendance of materialism, individualism, and competitiveness. As Astin (1993) has pointed out, "During the past forty or fifty years American universities have come to be dominated by three powerful and interrelated values: *materialism, individualism,* and *competitiveness*" (p. 4). One result of the ascendancy of these three values, continues Astin, is that "we have the scholars, to be sure, but we lack the community. One might more aptly characterize the modern university as a 'collection,' rather than a community of scholars" (p. 7). Astin's observations share kinship with Cushman's minimalist definition already cited of service-learning as the uniting of "the traditionally separate duties of research, teaching, and service."

Because the academy is intertwined with other institutions that comprise American culture, it is both a symptom and a cause of the problem of community fractured by materialism, individualism, and competitiveness. Hepburn (1997) traces the impact of this problem to the late 1980s, when "individuals found themselves increasingly disconnected from public life and civic discourse" (p. 140). Henson and Sutliff (1998) trace service-learning to "the attempts of some institutions of higher education to revitalize their moral and intellectual leadership in a democratic society" (p. 191). Thus, it seems fair to say that service-learning is a response to a perceived crisis in community.

This crisis in community presents a dilemma for higher education because higher education itself is one of the culprits that helped precipitate the crisis. Therefore, it must itself be revitalized morally and intellectually so that it can provide the education befitting citizens of a democracy. Although Mattson (1998) is skeptical about whether higher education ever really exerted the level of civic responsibility in the twentieth century that many proponents of service-learning say it did, those who advocate the civic approach to service-learning insist that the academy must be transformed to fit the impulse that drove John Dewey to promote "knowledge as a tool for creating a just society" (Hatcher, 1997, p. 24). Such knowledge will help create a society in which all citizens participate fully in political decision making. Only such full participation will eradicate the social evils—poverty and racism, to name just two—that are unmistakable blemishes on the national social landscape today.

It is not enough merely to add service to the curriculum, proponents of the civic approach affirm; they believe the philanthropic-additive approach does not go far enough to solve social problems and promote justice. Rather, the whole approach to education must be radically reformed. As Howard (1998) says, "Over time I have come to realize that to create a classroom that is consistent with the goals and values of service learning, it is absolutely necessary to deprogram or desocialize students and instructors away from traditional classroom roles, relationships, and norms, and then resocialize them around a new set of classroom behaviors" (p. 25). This program of resocialization, however, is inimical to the ethos of the academy as it now functions, for, as Harkavy and Benson (1998) note, the goal of service-learning should be to "overthrow the aristocratic Platonic theory of 'liberal education' and institute a democratic Deweyan theory of 'instrumental education'" (p. 19). Morrill (1982) makes a similar point: "The task of civic education is, then, especially difficult and ambitious for it involves the empowerment of persons as well as the cultivation of minds. This is not an undertaking for which contemporary colleges and universities are especially well equipped because many of the well-known features of modern collegiate education create serious barriers to a powerful civic education" (p. 365).

Marullo (n.d.) agrees with Morrill: "I will argue that service learning programs, if implemented properly, should be critical of the status quo and should ultimately challenge unjust structures and oppressive institutional operations" (p. 2). One implication of this criticism of the status quo is the "discrediting of the political economy that results from students discovering that it is the overt operations of market forces, aided by the political-economic system designed to generate inequality, that is responsible for the misery they see" (p. 13). Indeed, Rice and Brown (1998) affirm "the need to link service learning pedagogy with curriculum that introduces students to issues of personal and institutional power and oppression, in order to foster the development of self-reflective, culturally aware, and responsive community participants" (p. 146).

The focus on empowerment is not limited to students, who, proponents of the civic approach note, surely must be enabled to be change agents in a democratic society and oppose oppression of every sort. Professors also must change. They must come to see that a collaborative teaching style, which puts them in the place of learners so that they can identify with students, is critical if the pedagogy of service-learning is to transform the academy and, concomitantly, American culture at large. Neither the vocationalism that the academy has embraced nor the purist model of learning for learning's sake will meet this goal (Barber, 1993). There cannot be "large and impersonal classes, lack of context relevance, and lack of direct contact between students and faculty" (Cleary and Benson, 1998, p. 125). Instead, the classroom should become a place where equals meet and form communities based on mutual respect to support each other as they identify with communities outside the classroom—communities broken and bleeding because they have been oppressed and treated unjustly. In meeting in the classroom to provide a staging area for the offense against injustice, students and professors create a community that practices the values they will promote in the new society.

I have tried to represent the civic approach accurately, knowing that the continuum I spoke of earlier allows for various points of agreement closer to and further from the authors I have quoted. Nevertheless, in aggregate, the civic approach represents a significant voice in the service-learning movement, and professors will want to know not only what that approach offers to and requires of them, but also will want to know whether the service-learning movement as a whole has been successful in implementing its vision of a just academy that produces citizens ready to be change agents for justice. I now turn to evidence from those who have been implementing service-learning courses to provide information that professors can use to begin gauging the success of the service-learning movement to date and to gain insight into the issues that face those who implement a service-learning course.

The Success of Service-Learning Initiatives

Because service-learning is a relatively new pedagogy, we should not expect definitive answers about its effectiveness. In fact, Astin and Sax (1998) note, "To date, empirical studies on the impact of service are quite scarce" (p. 251). In addition, Eyler, Giles, and Braxton (1997) say, "There is very little empirical research to go along with the social and theoretical justification for service-learning, and what research there is has been mixed" (p. 5). Giles and Eyler (1998) affirm, "Faculty and administrators are intensely interested in this issue [of the relationship between service-learning and subject matter learning], but convincing evidence of the importance of service learning to subject matter learning is still lacking" (p. 67). These assertions about lack of definitive research to confirm the impulses that motivate service-learning and attest to the claims of those who support it do not mean that no research exists to give indications of service-learning's effectiveness or lack thereof.

In fact, Astin and Sax (1998), in reporting on a study they conducted, say, "The findings reported show clearly that participating in service activities during the undergraduate years substantially enhances the student's academic development, life skill development, and sense of civic responsibility" (p. 262). Eyler, Giles, and Braxton (1997) report in their study of service-learning, "Service-learning programs do appear to have an impact on students' attitudes, values, skills and the way they think about social issues even over the relatively brief period of a semester. These findings are even more consistent in arts and sciences classes. While the effect is significant, it is small; few interventions of a semester's length have a dramatic impact on outcomes" (p. 13). They note as well the need "to identify more clearly the types of service-learning experience that make the greatest difference to students" (p. 13), so a crucial aspect of service-learning needs further investigation.

Henson and Sutliff (1998), in reporting on their experience of integrating service-learning into a business and technical writing classroom, say, "Integrating service learning into a regular class stimulates both teaching and learning" (p. 201). Others agree that service-learning is beneficial (Rhoads, 1998; Rice and Brown, 1998).

Yet as Eyler, Giles, and Braxton (1997) noted, the results are mixed. For instance, Miller (1997) reports that one of the hypotheses of his study of college freshmen—"Students, over-all, will report an increased sense of the power of people to make a difference in the world"—was not confirmed. In fact, he found that "students perceived people to have less power than before the experience [of service-learning]" (p. 18). He nevertheless interprets this result positively because it represents a change in a particular group of students' unrealistic expectations about the level of their influence in helping to change the world. Koliba (1998), in reflecting on his case study of service-learning, identifies one of the problems he encountered as underuse of students in a redevelopment project: "Most . . . did not feel as if they were an integral part of the planning process, let alone members of the community. In most instances, there was never any dialogue between the students and the residents" (p. 83). Indeed, Neururer and Rhoads (1998), in considering the results from their study of graduate and undergraduate students engaged in service-learning, remark, "Community service, as a panacea to bridge class differences, as well as racial differences, falls apart upon close examination of our data" (p. 325).

These successes and failures suggest that more research needs to be done to determine the best ways to integrate service-learning into the curriculum and identify the types of activities best suited for meeting the goals of service-learning initiatives. For instance, Astin and Sax (1998) view tutoring and teaching as "by far the most common forms of education-related service" (p. 257). Yet Schutz and Gere (1998) question the use of tutoring as an effective means of achieving the goal of developing community among equals:

> The strength of tutoring as a mode of service is its ability to promote close individual relations between tutors and tutees. Yet, without a deep connection to a tutee's communities, the effort to create such a relation may be seriously constrained. Thus, it is not surprising that tutoring often fails to change college students' visions of their tutees as lacking a free-floating "expert" knowledge that they can provide. [p. 135]

In other words, tutoring maintains the status distinction between those who help and those who need help, one of the distinctions that the civic approach believes perpetuates injustice. Clearly, the research provides only a rough guide to professors who want to know how successful service-learning initiatives have been.

Objections to Service-Learning

Studies on the effectiveness of service-learning in courses suggest that professors will find challenges as they seek to implement this pedagogy. In particular, I address three major challenges or objections to service-learning: service-learning takes too much time and too many resources; it should not be required; and it should be resisted because it is a form of indoctrination.

• *Service-learning takes too much time and too many resources.* One of the immediate responses to the call for professors to participate in service-learning is that there is not enough time for professors to do everything they want to in a course. Thus, service-learning can be perceived as taking time away from the study of course content and requiring additional resources that could be used for other existing needs, such as increasing photocopying budgets. And that is true. Professors will not only spend more time than usual setting up service-learning in their classes but will also have to readjust their thinking about what constitutes effective education. They will need to reconsider the belief that stuffing students with content knowledge is the sole or the most important function of academic education.

In addition, professors who integrate service-learning into their classrooms will find that the relationship between the classroom and the organizational environments in which students engage in service is not necessarily tidy. Gordon (1999) notes that "working with a community partner can be a dance of accommodation" (p. 22). Sax and Aston (1997) not only endorse the idea that each campus should have a centralized service-learning center; they believe that without such a center, the necessary "level of coordination between faculty and community agencies will be nearly impossible to attain" (p. 32). Indeed, the costs for such a center can increase the resentment of professors who are struggling to live with inadequate budgets. In short, service-learning requires precious resources, including classroom time and a variety of support mechanisms.

Ultimately, the question to resolve is this: Are those resources well spent, or could they be better spent in other ways? Proponents of service-learning affirm that the resources are well spent, but questions about the effectiveness of resource allocations are notoriously difficult to answer unless good evaluative data are available. As I have noted, research results on the effectiveness of service-learning are mixed, and even the evaluation of individual students' efforts in a service-learning project can be inconclusive. For example, Eddy and Carducci (1997), in discussing the evaluation of students' writing in their service-learning class, admit that student writing "aims to, and often does, affect the local community in ways both subtle and profound, but difficult to estimate and evaluate" (p. 83).

• *Service-learning should not be required.* Another objection takes advantage of the seemingly ironic position that service-learning, which is intended to breed a long-lasting desire for voluntary service, can be required. This objection may be based on a misunderstanding of volunteerism as spontaneous. Indeed, volunteerism is no doubt a learned behavior that can be nurtured best in an environment where service is naturally accepted as part of a person's civic responsibility. Such environments, however, are not the norm, and although students might initially resist the notion of being required to serve as part of an academic class, they may learn that service is worth their energies and make it part of their postgraduation lifestyle (Carpenter and Jacobs, 1994). Again, however, whether service-learning should be required depends in part on what education is.

If Dickson (1979) is correct when he says, "Education does not mean teaching people to know what they do not know, it means teaching them to behave as they do not behave" (p. 149), then service-learning might very well be required.

One of the strongest arguments in favor of requiring service-learning comes from Schnaubelt and Watson (1999): "One could argue that forcing a student to do algebra homework also violates one's personal freedom. This imposition, however, may lead to greater freedom (i.e., admission to a good college, a better job, etc.). In a sense, some impositions lead to greater freedoms" (pp. 12–13). Indeed, their comments raise a more fundamental issue: Why is any course required? Certainly, professors believe they have the right to impose graduation requirements on students, in both the general education program and students' majors, so any argument against imposing requirements would need to explain why certain requirements are defensible and others are not.

• *Service-learning should be resisted because it is a form of indoctrination.* Perhaps the most potent argument against service-learning is that it appears, at least in the civic approach, to be indoctrination. Students *will* learn to be democratic citizens, and they *will* subscribe to particular political views about the evils of capitalism. The authors I have quoted who openly criticize the status quo certainly could be interpreted as pushing a particular agenda, one that is based on notions of human perfection, as was typical of Dewey's thought.

This qualm about a particular ideological impulse for service-learning, however, need not keep professors from engaging in it. After all, the continuum of service-learning impulses offers a variety of perspectives from which to integrate service-learning in higher education classrooms. And as Huckin (1997) notes, students can be given some flexibility in choosing service-learning projects: "It is important to let students choose the agency they want to work with, and to do so in full awareness of the kind of work the agency does and its governing philosophy or ideology. Many nonprofit agencies have strong political stances, and it might not be a good idea to have a right-to-life activist, for example, doing a project for Planned Parenthood" (p. 52).

In short, the purpose of service-learning in general is to integrate in the classroom the learning of concepts with the implementation of those concepts both inside and outside the classroom. The hope of service-learning is that when students participate in such an integrated course, they will choose as a lifelong goal to engage voluntarily in service.

Conclusion

Service-learning, like any other pedagogical initiative, presents risks and rewards attended by numerous barriers and pitfalls. Professors need to investigate both risks and rewards and be aware of pitfalls and barriers before committing themselves to service-learning. While the purpose of this book is to provide professors with nuts-and-bolts answers to practical issues related to service-learning, it is also imperative for professors to be aware of the impulses behind service-learning because theory drives practice.

References

Althaus, J. "Service-Learning and Leadership Development: Posing Questions Not Answers." *Michigan Journal of Community Service Learning,* 1997, *4,* 122–129.

Astin, A. W. "Higher Education and the Concept of Community." Fifteenth David Dodds Henry Lecture, University of Illinois at Urbana-Champaign, 1993. (ED 384 279)

Astin, A. W., and Sax, L. J. "How Undergraduates Are Affected by Service Participation." *Journal of College Student Development,* 1998, *39,* 251–263.

Barber, B. R. "The Civic Mission of the University." In B. R. Barber and R. Battistoni (eds.), *Education for Democracy.* Dubuque, Iowa: Kendall/Hunt, 1993.

Barber, B. R., and Battistoni, R. (eds.). *Education for Democracy.* Dubuque, Iowa: Kendall/Hunt, 1993.

Battistoni, R. "Service Learning and Democratic Citizenship." *Theory into Practice,* 1997, *36,* 150–156.

Bush-Bacelis, J. L. "Innovative Pedagogy: Academic Service-Learning for Business Communication." *Business Communication Quarterly,* 1998, *61,* 20–34.

Carpenter, B. W., and Jacobs, J. S. "Service Learning: A New Approach in Higher Education." *Education,* 1994, *115,* 97–99.

Cleary, C. "Steps to Incorporate Service Learning into an Undergraduate Course." *Journal of Experiential Education,* 1998, *21,* 130–133.

Cleary, C., and Benson, C. E. "The Service Integration Project: Institutionalizing University Service Learning." *Journal of Experiential Education,* 1998, *21,* 124–129.

Cushman, E. "The Public Intellectual, Service Learning, and Activist Research." *College English,* 1999, *61,* 328–336.

Dickson, A. "Altruism and Action." *Journal of Moral Action,* 1979, *8,* 147–155.

Eddy, G., and Carducci, J. "Service with a Smile: Class and Community in Advanced Composition." *Writing Instructor,* 1997, *16,* 78–90.

Eyler, J., Giles, D. E., Jr., and Braxton, J. "The Impact of Service-Learning on College Students." *Michigan Journal of Community Service Learning,* 1997, *4,* 5–15.

Forman, S. G., and Wilkinson, L. C. "Educational Policy Through Service Learning: Preparation for Citizenship and Civic Participation." *Innovative Higher Education,* 1997, *21,* 275–285.

Giles, D. E., Jr., and Eyler, J. "A Service Learning Research Agenda for the Next Five Years." In R. A. Rhoads and J.P.F. Howard (eds.), *Academic Service Learning: A Pedagogy of Action and Reflection.* New Directions for Teaching and Learning, no. 73. San Francisco: Jossey-Bass, 1998.

Gordon, R. "Problem-Based Service-Learning." *Academic Exchange Quarterly,* 1999, *3,* 16–27.

Harkavy, I., and Benson, L. "De-Platonizing and Democratizing Education as the Bases of Service Learning." In R. A. Rhoads and J.P.F. Howard (eds.), *Academic Service Learning: A Pedagogy of Action and Reflection.* New Directions for Teaching and Learning, no. 73. San Francisco: Jossey-Bass, 1998.

Hatcher, J. A. "The Moral Dimensions of John Dewey's Philosophy: Implications for Undergraduate Education." *Michigan Journal of Community Service Learning,* 1997, *4,* 22–29.

Henson, L., and Sutliff, K. "A Service Learning Approach to Business and Technical Writing Instruction." *Journal of Technical Writing and Communication,* 1998, *28,* 189–205.

Hepburn, M. A. "Service Learning in Civic Education: A Concept with Long, Sturdy Roots." *Theory into Practice,* 1997, *36,* 136–142.

Howard, J.P.F. "Academic Service Learning: A Counternormative Pedagogy." In R. A. Rhoads and J.P.F. Howard (eds.), *Academic Service Learning: A Pedagogy of Action and Reflection.* New Directions for Teaching and Learning, no. 73. San Francisco: Jossey-Bass, 1998.

Huckin, T. N. "Technical Writing and Community Service." *Journal of Business and Technical Communication,* 1997, *11,* 49–59.

Koliba, C. "Lessons in Citizen Forums and Democratic Decision-Making: A Service-Learning Case Study." *Michigan Journal of Community Service Learning,* 1998, *5,* 75–85.

Marullo, S. "The Service Learning Movement in Higher Education: An Academic Response to Troubled Times." [http://comm-org.utoledo.edu/si/marullo.htm]. N.d.

Mattson, K. "Can Service-Learning Transform the Modern University? A Lesson from History." *Michigan Journal of Community Service Learning,* 1998, *5,* 108–113.

Miller, J. "The Impact of Service-Learning Experiences on Students' Sense of Power." *Michigan Journal of Community Service Learning,* 1997, *4,* 16–21.

Mohan, J. "Thinking Local: Service-Learning, Education for Citizenship and Geography." *Journal of Geography in Higher Education,* 1995, *19,* 129–143.

Morrill, R. L. "Educating for Democratic Values." *Liberal Education,* 1982, *68,* 365–376.

Morton, K., and Saltmarsh, J. "Addams, Day, and Dewey: The Emergence of Community Service in American Culture." *Michigan Journal of Community Service Learning,* 1997, *4,* 137–149.

Neururer, J., and Rhoads, R. A. "Community Service: Panacea, Paradox, or Potentiation." *Journal of College Student Development,* 1998, *39,* 321–330.

Ogburn, F., and Wallace, B. "Freshman Composition, the Internet, and Service-Learning." *Michigan Journal of Community Service Learning,* 1998, *5,* 68–74.

Rhoads, R. A. "In the Service of Citizenship: A Study of Student Involvement in Community Service." *Journal of Higher Education,* 1998, *69,* 277–297.

Rice, K. L., and Brown, J. R. "Transforming Educational Curriculum and Service Learning." *Journal of Experiential Education,* 1998, *21,* 140–146.

Rosenberg, L. "Becoming the Change We Wish to See in the World: Combating Through Service Learning Learned Passivity." *Academic Exchange Quarterly,* 2000, *4,* 6–11.

Sax, L. J., and Astin, A. W. "The Benefits of Service: Evidence from Undergraduates." *Educational Record,* 1997, *78,* 25–33.

Schaeffer, M. A., and Peterson, S. "Service Learning as a Strategy for Teaching Undergraduate Research." *Journal of Experiential Education,* 1998, *21,* 154–161.

Schnaubelt, T., and Watson, J. L. "Connecting Service and Leadership in the Classroom." *Academic Exchange Quarterly,* 1999, *3,* 7–15.

Schutz, A., and Gere, A. R. "Service Learning and English Studies: Rethinking 'Public' Service." *College English,* 1998, *60,* 129–149.

BRUCE W. SPECK *is dean of the College of Arts and Sciences at the University of North Carolina at Pembroke.*

2

Creating a service-learning class need not be a daunting or protracted task. This chapter provides a simple seven-step model for service-learning success.

A Smart Start to Service-Learning

Maureen Shubow Rubin

Once upon a time, just as winter was beginning to chill the air, a rabbit looked up at the birds in the sky with wonder. Birds, he thought enviously, can fly south for the winter and need not worry about starving or freezing to death. He discussed the situation with a bird who was perched on a nearby branch.

"You are so lucky," the rabbit said. "You don't have to deal with winter. You can just follow the sunshine to a place where you can eat mangoes to your heart's content!"

"That's because I fly," said the bird.

"Cool," said the rabbit. "But how do you fly?"

"I can give you theory," the bird responded. "But implementation is your problem."

Many times higher education seems to bear an unfortunate philosophical resemblance to the rabbit in this opening tale. This chapter has no theory. It rests on the assumption that faculty members have been introduced to the benefits of service-learning for their teaching, student learning and personal growth, and the betterment of communities. It assumes that they, like the rabbit, want to learn the basics of implementation.

The Center for Community-Service Learning at California State University, Northridge, can provide all of the forms mentioned in this chapter. Many of these forms were adapted from the outstanding work of colleagues, especially the director of community service learning in the California State University Office of the Chancellor, California State University at San Marcos, San Francisco State University, and Azusa Pacific University. Downloading information is located on the Web site for the Center for Community-Service Learning at California State University, Northridge, www.csun.edu/~ocls99.

The course development model for launching successful service-learning classes has seven steps for faculty members (see Figure 2.1):

1. Define student learning outcomes.
2. Define personal scholarship outcomes.
3. Plan community collaboration.
4. Design the course.
5. Arrange logistics and create forms.
6. Reflect, analyze, and deliver.
7. Perform assessment and evaluation of and among all critical audiences.

These seven steps are presented as linear, but depending on the professor's existing community relations or history with other forms of experiential learning, the steps may not precisely follow the order in which they are presented. For example, Step 4, "design the course," may be done concurrently with or even prior to the previous steps. The important point is that all steps should be completed, although not necessarily in the strict order presented.

The companion piece to the course development model is the assignment and outcomes planner (see Exhibit 2.1), which is used to match classroom activities to desired student outcomes. These two com-

Figure 2.1. Service-Learning Course Development Model

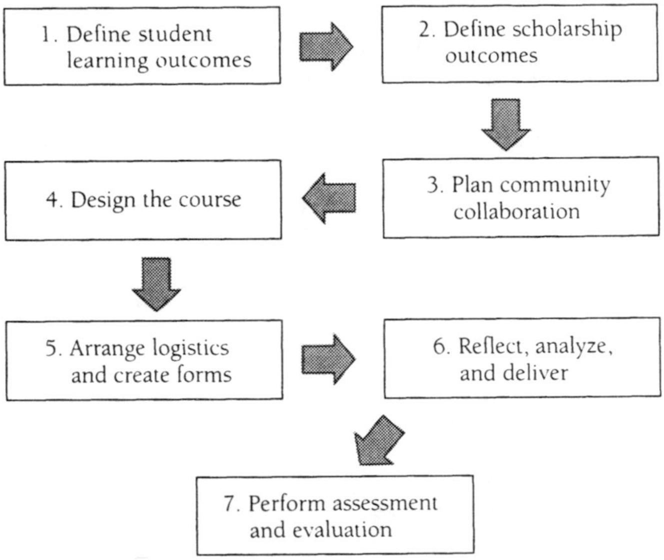

Source: Center for Community-Service Learning, California State University, Northridge. Reprinted by permission.

ponents work together to guide professors to match assignments with desired outcomes each week throughout the semester. As professors move through the course development model, they will integrate course assignments with desired outcomes at the end of each of the seven steps by filling out the planner. This planner will help the professor ensure that each selected outcome, indicated by the choices recorded on the top row of the chart (Student Learning, Scholarly Activity, and Service), receives adequate attention throughout the semester, as reflected in the assignments recorded in the vertical columns. When completed, the planner will immediately alert the professor to outcomes that do not have any supporting assignments. For example, if increasing awareness of community is chosen as a desired student learning outcome, the professor will see the need to plan specific assignments that expose students to the community before they perform their service. Lectures and readings could be assigned to help students understand community demographics, as well as key local issues in areas such as health, education, housing, and the economy, even if those areas are not normally associated with courses in the discipline. Not every learning outcome requires something in every assignment box. For example, in the Exam box under "awareness of community," the student learning outcome might well remain empty because that outcome might be better served by a series of reflection assignments. But if the entire vertical column below any outcome box remains vacant throughout the semester's plan, the professor might not be adequately preparing students for that desired learning outcome, and it probably will not be achieved. Let us take a closer look at each step in the course development model.

Exhibit 2.1. Assignment and Outcomes Planner

Week # _____					Outcomes			
	Student Learning			Scholarly	Service			
	1.	2.	3.	Activity	1.	2.	3.	
Assignments								
Lecture topic								
Reading								
Assignment								
Exam								
Reflection								
Analysis								
Deliverable								

Source: Driscoll, 1988.

Step One: Define Student Learning Outcomes

A service-learning class, like any other class, should begin with a decision about what the professor wants students to learn. Syllabi normally carry this decision under the *Course Objective* heading, which usually reads something like, "To develop a fundamental understanding of the course material, its theory, and its application." One of the main benefits of service-learning is its ability to expand student learning beyond this type of typical objective into a new range of learning outcomes that blend academic study with civic engagement and awareness, as well as practical experience.

Depending on the discipline and individual goals, choices of additional student learning outcomes include improving community awareness, involvement with community, commitment to service, career development, self-awareness, sensitivity to diversity, sense of ownership, communication skills, life skills, morality and character, and critical thinking and analysis (Driscoll and others, 1998). A psychology class, for example, may prioritize enhancing self-awareness and sensitivity to diversity, and a political science class may aim to increase students' awareness of community and their commitment to service.

Professors who are teaching a service-learning class should think broadly about student learning outcomes and consider the opportunity to teach values and commitments that might not typically be included in their discipline. One of the primary purposes of higher education, after all, is to train tomorrow's leaders and to instill in students a lifelong commitment to service, civic responsibility, and making a difference in the societal issues that relate to their communities and future work.

The faculty member should select two to three of these or additional student learning outcomes and record them on the top row of Exhibit 2.1 under the Student Learning heading. As the instructor moves through the model, the vertical boxes in the planner will help ensure that class material, readings, and assignments support the selected student learning outcomes.

Step Two: Define Personal Scholarship Outcomes

Faculty often report that they are reluctant to get involved in service-learning because doing it well requires additional time and effort that might not be recognized during retention, tenure, and promotion (RTP) procedures. Although many universities are rethinking traditional RTP paths, most still adhere to the "publish or perish" school of thought. As a result, a wise novice will integrate scholarship into service-learning courses with an eye toward publication in service-learning, education, or discipline-based journals.

Service-learning research can be done in two main ways. First, traditional discipline-based research can use service-learning classes to advance the knowledge of the field through use of the discipline's own research methodologies. A professor can work with students to gather data or test a theoretical concept in the community. Second, the service-learning class can be a laboratory for pedagogical research that tests the value of service-learning as a teaching and learning device. Research can also combine both.

Discipline-based research usually measures progress toward the traditional course objective of developing a fundamental understanding of the course material while advancing knowledge in the field. In an example of discipline-based research, Lenk (1997) looks at ways to maximize the professional preparation of future accountants. She describes a multisemester course that involves a partnership between upper-division accounting students and the state's professional accounting association. She also discusses the development and evolution of the strategic alliance that led to students' providing cost-effective consulting services for nonprofit organizations as part of their service-learning experience.

In pedagogical research, a professor can investigate many learning outcomes and related issues. Corbett and Kendall (1999), for example, examined students' service-learning experiences in courses taught in the communications department at the University of Utah. The authors looked at the relationship between student perceptions of their service-learning and better citizenship, a desirable student learning outcome.

In addition, a single service-learning project can lend itself to either pedagogical or discipline-based research. A psychology professor who specializes in gerontology on my campus has begun an interdisciplinary project with computer science students to teach computer skills to a group of senior citizens. Computer science students will teach these citizens to use the Internet, and gerontology students will help them overcome the fear of computers that is common in this age group. The gerontology students will pre- and posttest the senior citizens regarding their anxieties about working with computers and technology and then will conduct support groups and activities to raise their comfort levels. This project could result in a discipline-based article for a gerontology journal, discussing strategies for overcoming fear of technology in seniors, or it could result in a pedagogical publication about interdisciplinary service-learning teaching strategies for working with the elderly on technology projects.

When the scholarly outcomes are determined, the professor updates the assignment and outcomes planner with a desired scholarly activity outcome in the center of the top row. The vertical boxes below are a reminder to plan activities that match the instructor's research needs with class assignments throughout the semester.

Step Three: Plan Community Collaboration

At this point, the professor has created goals for both student learning and professional scholarship. Now it is time to choose a community partner and begin to create a true collaboration. Many professors already have a partner in mind, perhaps from supervising internships or sending students to volunteer with local programs. If the professor needs to identify appropriate sites, several campus resources should be able to help. The service-learning or volunteer office should have databases of local agencies that work with students. If there is no such resource, the professor should call United Way or a local politician to ask what community groups are working in the desired field. The professor can call a few potential partners, briefly describe ideas for collaboration with the service-learning class, and, if there is interest, make an appointment for a joint curriculum design session. This session should be held at the community site so the professor can understand the environment in which students will be serving. The session should also include a tour, introductions to key personnel involved in the collaboration, and ample time for an initial planning meeting. It is helpful to have a representative from the campus service-learning office along to facilitate the process.

In preparing for the initial session, the professor should realize that community representatives usually do not know what service-learning is or how it differs from volunteerism. Education is part of any successful collaboration. The community agency needs to understand that while it is appropriate for volunteers to file, paint, or pick up trash, such activities are rarely compatible with mastering course content. At the same time, the professor should heed Kellett and Goldstein's (1999) advice that "communities are well-developed, complex entities that must be understood and accepted rather than required to adapt to university culture" (p. 32). All too often, as Fertman (1993) writes, university and community agency staffs exist in parallel but separate worlds. They serve the same population but have different operating styles, priorities, practices, levels of professional training, theoretical bases, and even vocabulary. Each partner must understand and appreciate the perspectives, needs, and, especially, contributions of the other. There is no place for arrogant attitudes on the part of faculty members or students. Instead, everyone must recognize and respect the significant contributions of all partners as coeducators.

Following a simple plan at the initial meeting will lead to collaborative curriculum design. The professor can begin by asking the community partner to provide a few vital statistics—the agency's mission, main interest, population served, organizational structure, and budget—as well as how it addresses the major issues facing its target population. Next, he or she asks the community representative to provide three service outcomes that the agency would like students to accomplish. Then it is the faculty member's turn to describe the course in which service-learning will be used. Professors should explain what they want their students to learn and should be sure to identify their top three learning outcomes to ensure consistency between the partners.

At this point, the service outcomes and the learning outcomes may not match. On one occasion, for example, a professor teaching a course in microbiological hazards in environmental health in the department of health science met with representatives of a local environmental group to plan an appropriate service-learning project. Members of the community group wanted college students to clean a local dump. The professor explained that that activity was service, not service-learning, and that it was a more appropriate project for volunteers during a community cleanup day. He redirected the discussion by asking the group members to discuss some of their main environmental health concerns. Residents said they worried about septic tank spillage during seasonal rains. Dogs drank the surface water, and children played in it. The professor saw the link between their problem and his desired student learning outcomes. His students could test the water and write a scientific report on their findings. The community group could take it to local government officials to substantiate their concerns.

At the conclusion of the initial collaborative session, all participants should have identified several intersections where the goals of faculty and community partners coalesce. This curriculum design session is then repeated with additional community partners until enough sites are located to accommodate all students. The goal is to keep the number of placements at five or fewer to have time to communicate with and monitor all sites. Now is the time to update Exhibit 2.1 by recording service outcomes on the top row and making sure sufficient assignments are recorded in the boxes below to facilitate meaningful service and relate it to class materials.

Step Four: Design the Course

At this point, all outcomes are clarified. Obviously, there are many ways to design a course to achieve them. While it is useful to review sample syllabi for design ideas, remember that the first rule in designing a service-learning course is that there are no rules. Each professor must design an experience that furthers student learning outcomes, accomplishes the community partners' service outcomes, and complements the professor's scholarship goals. Following are five possible designs and descriptions of the courses in which they were employed (see also Florida International University, 1995).

- *Hypothesis testing.* In an upper-division public policy class, students were to question a fact or theory from the lecture or reading. One student chose to examine the contention that most recipients of assistance from AIDS-related social service agencies were middle- to upper-middle-class individuals rather than AIDS patients living below the poverty level. As the student helped to deliver care at the AIDS service agency, he simultaneously gathered demographic data on clients and found that most were indeed quite well off. He wrote a policy paper for the agency that included suggestions for improving outreach programs to target the city's indigent AIDS population better.
- *Teacher preparation.* Liberal studies or preteaching classes are natural fits for service-learning. Future teachers enrolled in classes such as "Physical Education for Children," "Art for Children," "Children's Literature," or

"Music for Children" have much to gain from testing classroom theories with children. After a period of observation, college students are given the opportunity to teach lessons and reflect on their success with input from peers, schoolteachers, and professors.

• *Multiple-semester projects.* Many times a community need cannot be addressed in a single semester. Professors can create multiple-semester projects that allow students to put a vital piece of the whole picture in place each semester. One health education professor, for example, was asked to plan school-based health fairs to provide basic health services and information (for example, on vaccinations, insurance information, and drug and alcohol abuse referrals). The professor created a three-semester plan. In the first semester, students did a community needs assessment. During the second semester, they surveyed local public and private resources that could address the identified needs. And in the third semester, they planned and implemented two health fairs at local schools.

• *Cross-disciplinary activities.* The health science professor in the multiple-semester project recruited professors and students from other disciplines, such as communicative disorders, kinesiology, and nursing, to create booths for the health fairs. In addition, students in a business class developed a marketing plan to increase campus involvement in the health fair project.

• *Project planning and execution.* Public relations students in their capstone course can design and implement fundraising and outreach projects for local nonprofit organizations. One such project saved the campus's aging orange grove from being bulldozed into a parking lot. Students joined with the local historical society to hold the Feeling Grovey Festival and obtained enough donations to buy new trees and irrigation equipment.

These examples illustrate some of the possibilities for course design. The design will facilitate syllabus construction, as week-by-week expectations are listed on the assignment and outcomes planner. The class syllabus must also totally integrate service-learning assignments. Too often, weekly assignments list lecture topics, readings, quizzes, and exams but relegate the service-learning components to a single paragraph at the end. This conveys an inaccurate picture of the relationship of service-learning to the course. It is not an afterthought. The Joint Educational Project at the University of Southern California recommends that service-learning course syllabi contain six key components (Cone, 2000):

1. A clear explanation of the connection between the academic content and the service component
2. Clearly stated course objectives related to the service
3. A description of the service requirements, including information on logistics that will be determined in Step Five

4. Specific information about placements, including names, addresses, and fairly detailed descriptions of participating community organizations

5. Clear information about requirements for reflection, critical analysis, or deliverable projects that will be determined in Step Six

6. A concise description of the evaluation process, including details on what will be evaluated and how the service experience will be weighed in the final grade

Step Five: Arrange Logistics and Create Forms

Now that the projects are agreed on, there is some nitty-gritty work to be done. Logistics are critical. Simple forms need to be developed to help professors with scheduling, carpooling, matching interests with tasks, time-keeping, and evaluation. Ideally the campus service-learning office will help with these vital tasks.

Before the initial meeting is over, professors and community partners should review a series of questions. Not all of them can be answered then, but tentative agreements should be reached on many, along with plans and timetables for answering the rest. Here are ten basic topics to address together:

- How long will the service component of the class last? What is the start date? End date?
- How many students will serve? How often? For how many hours?
- Are there transportation or parking problems?
- Who will conduct orientation for the college students? Will it be in-class or on-site orientation? Can community partners attend class during the first week to introduce their programs and answer student questions? What icebreakers will be used to break down barriers between students and their new clients?
- Who will be the on-site supervisor? What are the check-in and check-out procedures?
- How will students be evaluated? What outcome measures will be used to evaluate agency satisfaction with the students, and vice versa?
- How will communication among the faculty member, students, and community partners be maintained? Exchange home and work telephone numbers and e-mail addresses.
- What is the plan for closure and recognition of participants?
- Is any special training necessary prior to starting service? If so, can the faculty member and agency share the special training? When can it be scheduled?
- Are any additional tests or procedures, such as tuberculosis tests or fingerprinting, necessary prior to starting?

Step Six: Reflect, Analyze, and Deliver

Even if every service outcome the agency desires is achieved, a student's learning outcomes will not be met unless connections are made between the service performed and the course content. There are three primary ways to bring about these linkages: reflection, critical analysis, and deliverables.

Service-learning proponents agree that reflection is the most critical of the seven-step model, for it is the one that ties the service to the learning. There are many ways to help students reflect on their service-learning experiences. One of the most popular is requiring each student to keep a journal and make entries after each service experience. Some professors ask students to divide journal entries into three parts: facts, feelings, and relationship to course content. After each day of service, using different color inks or different computer fonts, students must write something related to each of the three areas. Many professors ask students to make journal entries on-line through a Web-based discussion forum that can be posted asynchronously for all to view and to make contributions. This format also allows professors to print entries and review them at their convenience. It is also possible to hold class sessions or office hours on-line to facilitate discussion groups.

Some professors require more detailed analyses. They ask specific questions that students must answer after each service session and require staggered papers throughout the semester. For example, after the first two sessions, the assignment could be to describe the site, explain what the students did, and describe the people they met. The third assignment could be a mini-analysis paper, to be completed after five hours of service. The paper could ask students to write about their first weeks and relate how they feel about what the agency is doing, what they find exciting, and what worries them. Similar sets of journal entries and papers continue throughout the semester.

The second type of linkage, analysis and critical thinking, ties specific on-site observations to questions and writing assignments related to course content. The questions will vary by discipline, but usually ask students to determine from on-site observations or conversations whether a course theory or concept is being demonstrated in the community's practice. If it is, the student should elaborate on how the theory is being applied. If it is not, the student should be asked to analyze whether the practice would be helped or hindered by application of the theoretical concept.

The last linkage is a deliverable—a product that is left in the community for its future use. Each of the course designs in Step Four lends itself to a deliverable. The AIDS researcher left a policy paper suggesting ways to increase outreach to the poor. Physical education students can prepare a series of age-appropriate lesson plans for use by teachers to increase children's motor development. Students planning health fairs can create directories of local health services. The deliverable often becomes a showcase for student creativity and academic achievement. Students also seem to try harder when they know the community will use the deliverable.

Professors should record reflection, critical analysis, deliverable assignments, and deadlines in the appropriate boxes on the assignment and outcomes planner and be careful to design assignments that genuinely help students link their learning to their service.

Step Seven: Perform Assessment and Evaluation

The last of the seven steps in the model is assessment and evaluation. Paloma and Banta (1999) explain, "Assessment is the systematic collection, review and use of information about educational programs undertaken for the purpose of improving student learning and development" (p. 4). It is formative and ongoing and should result in programmatic improvements after each semester. A university-wide assessment form should be developed and given to faculty to help them measure progress toward their own student learning and community service outcomes. In addition, all assessment forms should be returned to the service-learning office for university-wide review.

Assessment is simple to accomplish if it is tied to the student learning outcomes. Students' attitudinal and behavioral changes related to these outcomes can be measured by a variety of pre- and postcourse tests, such as surveys, interviews, or focus groups. It is important to create indicators that demonstrate changes in actual behavior as well as thought, or even wishful thinking. For example, faculty can measure student progress toward the awareness of the community outcome by asking students to mark a Likert scale from "strongly disagree" to "strongly agree" regarding a variety of statements. Under this outcome category, attitudinal changes can be measured by comparing pre- and posttest responses to questions such as, "The community in which our university is located is wealthy and has few problems with gangs, teenage pregnancy, and drug and alcohol use and abuse." Behavioral changes can be measured by comparing pre- and posttest responses to statements such as, "I regularly read newspapers to keep up with local issues."

Unlike assessment, evaluation is done by and for each service-learning population: students, faculty, and community sites. For example, students evaluate faculty and the service site through detailed questionnaires, and supervisors at the service site evaluate the students and their faculty partners using a checklist with space for comments. Specific forms are designed to glean vital information from each. For example, community partners can rank students from "unsatisfactory" to "excellent" in such areas as attendance and punctuality, quality of performance, respect for confidentiality, enthusiasm, and benefit of service provided. Students can rank their service experience from "very satisfied" to "very dissatisfied" in such areas as helpfulness of staff, adequacy of training and supervision, and meaningfulness of the tasks they performed.

All evaluation forms provide vital information to faculty members and the service-learning office that will be useful in improving course design and student placements.

Conclusion

This introduction to service-learning pedagogy, coupled with the other chapters in this book, should give novice practitioners help on what needs to be done to launch a successful and meaningful service-learning class. Service-learning is not an exact science, however. We often learn more from our failures than from our successes.

References

Cone, D. "Service Learning: Designing Course Syllabi." Joint Educational Project, University of Southern California. [http://www.usc.edu/dept/LAS/JEP]. 2000.

Corbett, J., and Kendall, A. "Evaluating Service Learning in the Communication Discipline." *Journalism and Mass Communication Educator,* 1999, 4(53), 66–76.

Driscoll, A. "Course Alignment Grid." Seaside: Center for Teaching, Learning and Assessment, California State University, Monterey Bay, 1998.

Driscoll, A., Gelmon, S., Holland, B., Kerrigan, S., Spring, A., Grosvold, K., and Longley, M. *Assessing the Impact of Service Learning: A Workbook of Strategies and Methods.* (2nd ed.) Portland, Oreg.: Center for Academic Excellence, Portland State University, 1998.

Fertman, C. "Making School-Agency Collaboration Work." *Education Digest,* 1993, *58,* 58–62.

Florida International University. "101 Ideas for Combining Service and Learning." [www.fiu.edu/~time4chg/Library/ideas.html]. June 27, 1995.

Kellett, C., and Goldstein, A. "Transformation in the University and the Community: The Benefits and Barriers of Collaboration." *Journal of Family and Consumer Services,* 1999, *91,* 31–35.

Lenk, M. "Discipline-Specific Knowledge in Service-Learning: A Strategic Alliance Amongst Universities, Professional Associations, and Non-Profit Organizations." *Michigan Journal of Community Service Learning,* 1997, 4, 104–108.

Paloma, C., and Banta, T. *Assessment Essentials.* San Francisco: Jossey-Bass, 1999.

MAUREEN SHUBOW RUBIN *is professor of journalism and director of the Center for Community-Service Learning at California State University, Northridge.*

3

Service-learning is an effective pedagogy to help ensure success for all students, including individuals with disabilities.

Service-Learning Is for Everybody

Robert Shumer

Almost three-quarters of two-year and four-year postsecondary institutions enroll students with disabilities (U.S. Department of Education, 2000). College initiatives recognize the need in the disabled community for service and for learning, and they promote the notion that service and individuals with disabilities are good for one another. Interestingly, though, the disabled populations most often served by college students lie primarily outside postsecondary institutions and are most frequently served by college students without disabilities. Nevertheless, this situation is improving. It is clear that college and individuals with disabilities go well together.

The Americans with Disabilities Act

The participation of individuals with disabilities in higher education has grown in the past decade, primarily as a result of passage of the Americans with Disabilities Act in 1990 and the more current (1997) amendments to the Individuals with Disabilities Education Act (IDEA). This legislation promotes inclusion of special individuals in mainstream life activities. At the beginning of the 1990s, almost half of the individuals with disabilities attending postsecondary education went to community colleges. One-quarter were in four-year public institutions, and 14 percent were in private, not-for-profit

The Center for Community-Service Learning at California State University, Northridge, can provide all of the forms mentioned in this chapter. Many of these forms were adapted from the outstanding work of colleagues, especially the director of community service learning in the California State University Office of the Chancellor, California State University at San Marcos, San Francisco State University, and Azusa Pacific University. Downloading information is located on the Web site for the Center for Community-Service Learning at California State University, Northridge, www.csun.edu/~ocls99.

institutions. Another 14 percent were in other settings. By the middle of the decade, approximately 6 percent of all undergraduates reported having a disability. The single largest group was learning disabled (29 percent), followed by students with orthopedic disabilities (23 percent), students with other health-related disabilities (21 percent), hearing-impaired students(16 percent), and visually impaired students (16 percent) (U.S. Department of Education, 1999).

How many students with disabilities are engaged in service-learning is unclear. Because many special needs individuals are mainstreamed into regular courses, the tendency is to undercount those who are actually doing service because many faculty and program coordinators are unaware of the disabled students who are participating in their service-learning experiences. The best data come from programs that tend to target individuals with special needs; hence their involvement is tracked as part of their course.

About 50 percent of community colleges and 30 percent of public and private four-year colleges offer service-learning (Shumer and Cook, 1999). Nevertheless, a review of the National Service-Learning Clearinghouse database, as well as the Educational Resources Information Center system, revealed few programs that involve special needs individuals in service-learning initiatives. It did reveal a larger number of programs that serve disabled communities, most of which are connected to programs for nondisabled college students that serve individuals with disabilities in public schools, community institutions, or community agencies.

One interesting finding is that students with disabilities perform more volunteer work than nondisabled students do. According to a 1995–1996 study, 32.3 percent of nondisabled students report volunteering, with 68 percent of them volunteering from one to five hours per week and 19 percent volunteering more than ten hours per week. Of students who report having disabilities, 39.2 percent report doing volunteer work, with 64 percent volunteering from one to five hours per week and 20 percent serving more than ten hours per week (U.S. Department of Education, 1996). If individuals with disabilities are in fact volunteering at rates greater than the general population, then not providing service-learning opportunities misses an excellent opportunity to connect their college education with service. Perhaps this is the most important message of the investigation: because special populations are already serving their communities, they need to be connected to academic programs through service-learning courses.

A great challenge in the next decade is providing college-level service-learning courses and programs for individuals with disabilities so they can contribute even more to the entire community.

Individuals with Disabilities as Recipients of Service

The majority of programs at the college level involving individuals with disabilities provide service to these individuals. From tutoring to mentoring, and academic assistance to personal development, programs in community and technical colleges and four-year institutions are predominantly service-learning efforts on the part of nondisabled college students who are serving special populations, who often are not located at the higher education institution.

These programs have shown an impact. For example, a study of college students participating in an occupational therapy program serving senior citizens (ages sixty-five to eighty-five) and disabled individuals (ages eighteen to fifty) found that the students developed a significant "other" orientation to the world, moving toward more empathy and understanding (Greene, 1998). College students who visited individuals with disabilities learned to appreciate the daily challenges they faced and to respect their ability to manage everyday activities. They also learned to honor them as individuals, acknowledging their personal strengths and their ability to have successes in life.

In another dual study, service-learning courses positively affected the attitudes of college students toward mental retardation. In the first situation investigated, students enrolled in a course on the psychology of mental retardation and did their service in day treatment programs, integrated day care, and residential home settings. They kept journals and completed a questionnaire about their community experiences. Analysis of the material showed that students formed positive attitudes about the experience and toward people with mental retardation. Students stated that the service project was a good idea. More than 80 percent found that "people with retardation were similar to themselves," and more than 25 percent found that "people with mental retardation were more capable than they had believed prior to their first-hand experiences" (Curran, 1998, p. 9).

In a second part of the same study, attitudes of students in the psychology class were compared with students in a non-service-learning course that dealt with consumer economics. On the pretest, there were no significant differences between the two groups on three of four measures. After the course, "attitudes of students who completed the [service-learning] course changed significantly" (Curran, 1998, p. 11). There were at least two important findings: students were more positive toward empowerment of individuals with disabilities and were less inclined toward sheltering them (Curran, 1998). These results indicate that when students work with developmentally disabled individuals, they learn to respect the abilities of that population. These attitudinal changes help to ensure that members of the mentally retarded community are treated with respect, a sense of accomplishment, and an understanding that comes from spending time interacting with them in their home environment. "Both studies support a positive trend toward the basic rights for those with mental retardation" (Curran, 1998, p. 11). As with the Greene study, service-learning experiences lead to a richer understanding of the daily lives of human beings who meet life's challenges in admirable and respectful ways.

Given the potential impact of working with disabled populations, many program models demonstrate the mutual benefit for college students and the special populations they serve. Perhaps one of the best overall models, and one of the oldest, is the Developmental Disability Immersion Program (DDIP) at the University of California at Los Angeles. Initiated in the late 1970s as a residential education program operated at a state hospital for people with developmental disabilities (containing an on-site research center and residential dormitories for students and patients), the program evolved in the 1980s and 1990s into an urban program. Students did their service-learning at either the state hospital or local special education programs near the campus.

The two-quarter program comprises the full academic schedule for students. They take basic courses in mental retardation, as well as courses in writing, research, fieldwork, and related psychology classes. The goal of the initiative is to help college students learn about disabled populations by working directly with them, providing service and support in the process.

The strength of the DDIP is its focus on academic learning, service, and research. Students take academic courses on content and research methods and are expected to complete a research project (working with a sponsor) on a topic related to mental retardation. The research ranges from biological studies to studies of behavior and training. The study and research culminates in a series of articles that are published annually in the *Pacific States Archives,* a research journal produced by undergraduates in the psychology department.

DDIP embodies all the important elements of good service-learning: meaningful service, integration into the academic curriculum, and research that supports the services for the clients and results in informative articles that are shared outside the setting. Few other programs around the country embody such well-integrated theory with practice and instruction informed by research.[1]

Students in textiles and clothing courses at West Virginia University provide service to special populations through a service-learning program. The course, "Clothing for Special Needs," requires students to focus on a variety of issues: "apparel design problems for individuals with functional limitations; marketing issues, such as availability and accessibility of functional apparel; and educational problems, such as teaching dressing skills to a person with a physical disability" (McDonald, 1994, p. 40). In one project for the class, a student developed an entire clothing selection and wardrobe maintenance system for a blind individual. The student helped the man to identify and code clothing, coordinate outfits, select appropriate fabrics, and actually purchase clothing to provide for a balanced wardrobe. These activities were tied to the academic content of the course through journal writing, construction of related bibliographies, and evaluation of the project by community members affected by the program.

Students in the program write a research paper based on their project and make oral presentations about the literature and the work. The service activities and related work constitute 60 percent of the total grade.[2]

The University of Utah includes service-learning in its course on human exceptionality, "Introduction to Special Education." To comply with the field placement component, students often work with local special education programs in schools or community agencies that serve special populations. A few work with neighbors or relatives. Projects are designed to connect the student's academic discipline to the needs of the disabled individuals served. For example, dance majors teach movement skills to blind students, an architecture student designs and builds a ramp for a family with a child using a wheelchair, and recreation and leisure students frequently volunteer at local camps for disabled children. In all cases, the community work is connected with the academic content of the course, with students documenting the increased understanding of the disability addressed and explaining how the service experience improves their understanding of human exceptionality.[3]

Florida State University includes service-learning in "Introduction to Mental Retardation." Students are required to spend a minimum of twenty hours getting to know an individual in the community with mental retardation. Through structured, reflective reports, students examine their attitudes toward mental retardation, as well as the conditions that involve living with developmental disabilities. Evaluation of the program, using reflective reports and several different instruments, documents the attitudinal change that occurs in the students. As a result of their service experiences in the community, college students positively change their views on what it means to be mentally retarded. The attitudinal changes reflect renewed respect and admiration for the disabled community members.[4]

Individuals with Disabilities as Service Providers

Relatively few programs include individuals with disabilities who provide service as part of their educational programs, but the number is growing, and the quality of the experiences is improving. One area of difficulty that some coordinators cite is that students with disabilities can be difficult to place. Sometimes the nature of the community task is not easily adaptable to an individual with a specific disability. Yet in other settings, the specific disability proves to be an asset.

At Metropolitan State University in St. Paul, Minnesota, the America Reads program, which focuses on literacy issues, requires field placements in community educational programs. The community coordinator for the program developed a special placement to accommodate the skills of a deaf college student who wanted to work in a program as a tutor using American Sign Language (ASL). She worked at a school for the deaf and tutored students in reading, using ASL. She received credit through a writing course that focused on literacy issues. Her paper on deafness as an educational challenge connected her fieldwork with students to the content of the course.[5]

Students in personal development classes at Southwestern College, in Chula Vista, California, do service-learning as part of their educational program. One of the more popular options is working with the Equestrian Therapy for the Handicapped program, in which individuals with disabilities from the college provide specific assistance to disabled participants. The college students help to teach the participants how to groom and tack their horses. College students use these experiences for discussion, reading, and writing in their class.[6]

Johnson County Community College, in Overland Park, Kansas, provides opportunities for individuals with special needs to serve others through a variety of courses. Their placements are often in other special needs settings, among them therapeutic day care and training settings, special education classes (K-12), sheltered workshops and group homes for older individuals, and therapeutic riding schools. College students with disabilities often provide direct services to their counterparts in the school system. A college student with learning disabilities might work with a student with a similar disability in the traditional school.[7]

Practical Advice: Developing Service-Learning Programs for College Students with Disabilities

All programs must be tailored to the characteristics and culture of specific institutions. The following suggestions should make the process easier:

• Find out what others have done and are doing to involve individuals with disabilities in service-learning initiatives. Besides the National Service-Learning Clearinghouse (1–800–808–7378; serve@tc.umn.edu; www.umn.edu/~serve) and the various programs mentioned in this chapter, many resources can answer questions and provide materials for curriculum, assessment, and program development. The National Service-Learning Exchange (LSAEXCHANGE@nylc.org) can provide information about people who might help meet program needs. The Academy for Educational Development in Washington, D.C. (www.aed.org and www.nichcy.org), and the Institute for Community Integration at the University of Minnesota (www.ici.umn.edu) are outstanding resources for people working in the world of disabilities.

• Contact other faculty at the institution who appear interested in linking their academic courses with community connections. It is often easier to start with people who believe in this kind of education and leave the skeptics and opponents for later. Develop solid programs with allies first; then win the others over with data after the program has become a success. Other faculty often listen to their peers, so plan to expand the program through faculty connections.

• Choose an approach to identify individuals or programs that focus on people with disabilities. The more traditional route is to focus on nondisabled college students who are serving special populations in their community. This amounts to discovering where special populations are receiving their education or where individuals with disabilities are clustered in the community, so that service-learning can be planned. Initiatives can be developed that connect the college students and their learning to serving the special populations, ensuring that the service provided is appropriate and necessary and is linked to academic courses.

The more direct approach is to focus on students in the institution who have disabilities. Seek out programs that serve them directly to make contact, or work with the institution's disabilities services office to identify places on campus where these students are found. Develop relationships with people in these programs. Often the disabilities services office works through courses to link course content to service activities.

• Develop the academic community connections necessary to support the service-learning initiative. Individuals with disabilities are already engaging in community service, so locate where they are doing service and determine how that service can be incorporated into the service-learning program.

Conclusion

Opportunities in college are expanding for individuals with disabilities. Not only is their participation rate in service-learning programs increasing, but also their engagement in these programs is on the rise. As service-learning programs expand in colleges, opportunities become more prevalent for individuals with disabilities to participate more fully in them.

With this increase in participation, there is an even greater opportunity to tap into the strong commitment to volunteering found in the disabled population. Almost 40 percent of disabled college students perform volunteer work. The challenge for higher education faculty and administration is to turn these experiences into more service-learning opportunities, allowing the disabled to learn even more from their community connections and potentially provide even more direct service to the noncollege disabled population, increasing the chance for everyone to lead fulfilled lives.

Notes

1. For information about the DDIP initiative, contact Bob Emerson, director of the Center for Experiential Education and Service-Learning at UCLA (remerson@soc .ucla.edu).

2. For information about the "Clothing for Special Needs" course, contact Nora MacDonald at the Division of Family Resources, West Virginia University (www.caf.wvu /famr/faculty.html).

3. For more information about this program, contact Jack Mayhew in the Department of Special Education (Mayhew@GSE.utah.edu).

4. For more information on this program and the current evaluation efforts under way, contact Bruce Menchetti (bmenchet@garnet.acns.fsu.edu).

5. Contact Susan Giguere (susan.giguere@metrostate.edu) for more information about placing individuals with disabilities in community-based learning programs.

6. For more information about this program, contact Silvia Cornejo-Darcy (scornejo @swc.cc.ca.us).

7. For specific information about these projects, contact Marcia Shideler (shideler @johnco.cc.ks.us).

References

Curran, J. "College Students' Attitudes Towards Mental Retardation: A Pilot Study." Paper presented at the 106th Annual Meeting of the American Psychological Association (San Francisco, Calif., August 14–18, 1998).

Greene, D. "Student Perceptions of Aging and Disability as Influenced by Service Learning." *Physical and Occupational Therapy in Geriatrics,* 1998, *15,* 39–55.

McDonald, N. "Service Learning in Undergraduate Textiles and Clothing." *Journal of Family and Consumer Sciences,* Winter 1994, pp. 39–44.

Shumer, R., and Cook, C. *The Status of Service-Learning in the U.S.: Some Facts and Figures.* St. Paul: National Service-Learning Clearinghouse, University of Minnesota, 1999.

U.S. Department of Education, National Center for Education Statistics. *1995–96 National Postsecondary Student Aid Study.* Undergraduate Data Analysis System. Washington, D.C.: U.S. Department of Education, National Center for Education Statistics, 1996.

U.S. Department of Education, National Center for Education Statistics. *Students with Disabilities in Postsecondary Education: A Profile of Preparation, Participation, and Outcomes.* Washington, D.C.: U.S. Department of Education, National Center for Education Statistics, 1999.

U.S. Department of Education, National Center for Education Statistics. *Postsecondary Students with Disabilities: Enrollment, Services, and Persistence.* Washington, D.C.: U.S. Department of Education, National Center for Education Statistics, 2000.

ROBERT SHUMER *is director of the National Service-Learning Clearinghouse and codirector of the Center for Experiential Education and Service-Learning at the University of Minnesota.*

4

Reflection exercises conducted before, during, and after service-learning projects can dramatically improve student learning.

Creating Your Reflection Map

Janet Eyler

Reflection is the hyphen in service-learning; it is the process that helps students connect what they observe and experience in the community with their academic study. In a reflective service-learning class, students are engaged in worthwhile activity in the community, observe, make sense of their observations, ask new questions, relate what they are observing to what they are studying in class, form theories and plans of action, and try out their ideas. The importance of this cycle of action and reflection, of intentional examination of experience, has long been central to practitioner wisdom in the field (Honnet and Poulsen, 1989; Mintz and Hesser, 1997). Growing empirical evidence supports the usefulness of students' analyzing their field experience. Conrad and Hedin's (1980) pioneering study with high school students noted the importance of program quality, including systematic discussion for positive student outcomes. Recent research in higher education has provided considerable additional evidence that quality makes a difference. The most important component of a high-quality program is frequent attention to the reflective process (Eyler, Giles, and Gray, 1999). And while service itself has a positive effect on personal development, if the objectives of service-learning include such cognitive goals as deeper understanding of subject matter, critical thinking, and perspective transformation, intensive and continuous reflection is necessary; little change is produced by classes that have community service as an add-on poorly integrated into the course (Eyler and Giles, 1999). Unfortunately, minimal or sporadic attempts to integrate service into the course are fairly typical of service-learning classes.

Students also stress the importance of reflection in adding value to their service-learning courses. In an exploratory study of reflective techniques in service-learning, sixty-six college students were interviewed about their experiences with volunteer service and service-learning (Eyler, Giles, and Schmiede, 1996). Students who had been involved with service-learning, in which service and learning were linked through reflective activities, were more likely than their volunteer peers to identify learning as an important outcome of their experience. They identified several important principles that made reflection effective for them. First, reflection should be continuous and not just an assignment or two at the end of a course. Second, reflection needs to connect course content and the community experience explicitly. Third, reflection should be challenging, forcing students to confront their own assumptions and pursue hard questions. Finally, they believed that different contexts called for different types of reflective activities. When possible, reflection should be integrated naturally into the projects and the course and not be viewed as an add-on activity.

Creating or borrowing reflection activities for service-learning classes is not difficult to do, but taking the time to plan systematically for reflection appears to be rare. The reflection map, which contains some sample activities, is a tool to help practitioners organize their thinking about integrating continuous reflective processes into their service-learning practice (Table 4.1). One dimension is the context for reflection—alone, with the class or group, and with the community partner. The second dimension is chronology—before, during, and after service. By focusing on filling each cell of the map during their course planning, instructors can be prepared to challenge their students with continuous reflection.

This chapter describes a number of activities designed to help students reflect in these various ways. (Most of these activities are from Eyler, Giles, and Schmiede, 1996.)

Reflection Before Service

One of the goals of reflective practice in service-learning is to help students become aware of their own assumptions and develop the habit of questioning themselves and others. Before students can challenge their own beliefs about the world, they need to know what they believe about the community, the issues, the people they will work with, and themselves. Asking students to bring to the surface some of these thoughts in an explicit way before they perform their initial service may serve as both a benchmark for later reflection and an exercise that heightens their awareness of the frames of reference that they bring to the new experience. From the beginning, they may experience their service in a more reflective way.

Creating Activities for Reflection Alone. Asking students to explore their expectations and assumptions individually helps prepare them for later class activities designed to stimulate inquiry. One idea for accomplishing this is an activity called *letter to myself*. Students are asked to create a document that they will send to themselves and not open until the end of the service placement or project. A set of questions appropriate to the experi-

Table 4.1. Mapping Service-Learning Reflection

	Activities Before Service	Activities During Service	Activities After Service
Reflection alone	Letter to myself	Structured journals	Reflective essay
Reflection with classmates	Hopes and fears Giant Likert scale	Service-learning theater Mixed team discussion	Team presentation Collage or mural Video
Reflection with community partners	Planning with community Asset mapping	Lessons learned, debriefing	Presentation to community group

ence and the academic goals of the course should be provided to help structure the letter. For example, students may be asked to describe what they expect the people they will be working with to be like, what their own contributions will be, and what they will see in the community. If the focus of the class includes exploration of social problems, they may be asked to discuss the sources of these problems and possible solutions.

When opened and read weeks later, this letter can be an interesting focus for a personal essay on the journey the student has undertaken in understanding the community, or it may serve as the basis for class discussion of what students have learned during the semester. It is common for students to be unaware of the changes in their thinking over the course of a semester of service-learning because the process may be gradual; seeing their preconceptions can trigger some interesting insights about the experience.

Creating Activities for Reflection with Classmates. Classroom preparation for community service is often focused on logistics and sometimes on training in the skills that will be needed at the service site. However, it is important to prepare students substantively for their service experience as well. Just as encouraging individual exploration of preconceptions prepares the student to be a more thoughtful participant, group activities to "preflect" on the planned service and its possible relationship to the academic study can generate curiosity that the academic portions of the course can help satisfy. The process can also be used to facilitate team planning for service-related activity and inquiry.

One activity to encourage students to begin to think about what they want to know is a brainstorming session on hopes and fears they have for the service experience. Students list these on flip charts and then explore what they need to do to address their fears or realize their hopes. One class studying public policy and soon to embark on an alternative spring break project with an outreach organization working in the area of acquired immunodeficiency syndrome identified one fear as their own parents' concern about their service with people living with human immunodeficiency virus (HIV). The group identified the specific concerns their parents had expressed and the group's inability to respond to these concerns; this discussion helped the group members to recognize some of their own fears and gaps in their knowledge. They then organized themselves to research some of the issues and drafted a letter to send to their parents detailing their training, safety precautions, and facts they had learned about transmissibility of HIV. This exploration of their own hopes and fears and their parents' concerns was a springboard for substantive preparation for their experience.

Another reflective activity that can challenge assumptions and provoke curiosity about the issues related to the community placement is a giant Likert scale. Preparation of the scale is accomplished by creating a series of statements related to the service or the academic subject matter of the course. Likert anchors ranging from Strongly Disagree to Strongly Agree are posted on classroom walls, and students physically place themselves where they belong in response to each of the statements. Following are some of the items used with students about to embark on service projects for their education policy class:

"Teachers in inner-city schools are less competent and caring than teachers in suburban schools."
"Voucher plans would allow any child to attend the private school of his or her choice."
"Students who fail in school usually have parents who don't care much about their progress."
"The most common time for juveniles to commit burglaries and other property crimes is after 11 P.M."

Often groups of students cluster at both the Agree and Disagree polls, and dialogue can be fostered on the spot. Students can then do some preliminary research on these issues and share their findings with the class. This exercise is fun for participants, illuminates assumptions that students bring to the study of the issue, and ignites curiosity, thus preparing students to observe more closely in the community and pursue answers in the library.

Creating Activities for Reflection with Community Partners. Reciprocity is central to effective service-learning, (Honnet and Poulsen, 1989; Sigmon, 1996), yet genuine joint planning of service projects to meet community needs is rare in service-learning classes. We know that interaction with community members contributes to positive student outcomes, but planning for reflection between students and community participants is a challenge. When this sort of reflection is possible, the instructor should create opportunities for students to engage in exploring needs with community members and engage in some mutual planning of the service activity. If this is not feasible for the entire class, sometimes it can be managed by designating student representatives. Sometimes a community project can stretch over several semesters, with the first team of students planning with the community and then handing off implementation to the next team.

A specific activity that can be conducted with community members and students is community asset mapping (McKnight and Kretzman, 1997). Those engaged in service often concentrate on the negatives about the community, that is, its problems and needs. McKnight and Kretzman argue that it is sometimes more fruitful to think about the strengths or assets of communities. They suggest a process of identifying institutions, associations, individuals, and other positive resources that the community can contribute toward development. This exercise can be the basis for planning a collaboration between student and community groups. It is also a tool that helps students understand that the way a question is framed influences what they observe.

Reflection During Service

Ideally students engage in ongoing reflection throughout their service. Most service-learning classes, particularly those in which only some students are participating in a service option, do not devote a lot of time to discussion of the experiences in the field. It is important to build this process into the class in ways that support course objectives.

Creating Activities for Reflection Alone. Given the demands on classroom time, it is important to create activities to ensure that students do a good deal of thinking about the connections between service and course work on their own. Self-monitoring of the learning process is important for cognitive development. A common choice for individual reflection is the student journal. Some students spontaneously create highly reflective journals, but many others view it as a burden and write either simple descriptive material about where they went and what they did or express their feelings about the events. (Undoubtedly some gather up a handful of different pens and try to create something the night before they turn in their journals.) To push students to observe clearly, raise questions, and make connections continually, instructors should provide some structure for this process and also provide frequent feedback. The journal can be structured many ways around issues emerging in the classroom, but it is useful to provide a few questions that will form a basic template for each entry. For example, early in their service experience, students might be asked: "What were your first impressions? What did you see and hear? Were you surprised by anything you saw? What questions do you have as a result of your experience today?" Later in the service, students can be asked to identify critical incidents and discuss how conflicts were resolved or problems overcome. And as the semester unfolds, they will be able to connect theories from the classroom with their field experiences.

At minimum, students need to describe their experiences in the community, react to those experiences, try to make sense of the experience in the context of what they are learning or have previously learned, and discuss implications for action. This is the well-known "What? So What? Now What?" process based on Kolb's (1984) cycle of action and reflection. For example, the "Now What?" component may well be questions that need to be answered or perhaps a strategy for doing something different the next time at the community site. These three questions can serve as the basic template for journal writing when other tasks are not assigned.

Instructors who set reflective tasks for the journal and read and respond to them should encourage students to take this process seriously. A structured journal is valuable in two distinct ways. By explicitly linking experience to the course of study, it challenges the student to be thoughtful. Furthermore, it provides a database the student can use to reflect on the entire experience at the end of the service-learning class. Students are often surprised as they read over their journals at how much their thinking about the community and issues changed over the semester. Journals both propel and record this growth. They also provide instructors with a way to monitor experiences and intervene when necessary and, of course, to provide feedback and challenge to students.

Creating Activities for Reflection with Classmates. It is important to create a series of activities over the course of a semester to help students integrate their experiences with their academic course of study. The most obvious reflective technique is the class discussion. The "What? So What? Now What?" structure can be used to help push discussion beyond sharing reactions and observations to linking those observations to course content and future action. Students can also take turns facilitating these discussions.

Service-learning theater is another activity that can engage students. The instructor invites students to construct and enact role-play scenarios around critical incidents from their community service. Classmates then explore the issue, apply insights from their study, and suggest a resolution to the critical incident or draw lessons from it. The critical incidents can be based on specific problems that students experience, such as difficulties in a mentor relationship with a teenager or in planning a community event. They can also be based on situations that the student observes in the field placement, such as the strategies that some recipients of service use to obtain service more effectively or how agencies bend regulations to provide needed service. Students may be invited to construct these incident descriptions in their journals or as written assignments. The instructor can select several journal entries that showcase different issues and concepts relevant to the subject matter of the course. Or students may work in teams to choose an illuminating incident to present.

Some classes make community service an optional assignment. This presents challenges for the instructor, and typically the service component is managed much as a term paper with little integration into the class. One way to integrate the experience of students doing community service with those engaged in more traditional library research is to create classroom teams with representatives from each group. These mixed teams can be assigned discussion topics that require them to share their expertise. For example, one team of researchers contributed their facts and figures about welfare reform, while those working in a community program for single mothers who were returning to work shared their experiences with families trying to cope with the implementation of those reforms.

Creating Activities for Reflection with Community Partners. Moore (1999) and others have observed that reflection does not necessarily happen spontaneously for students in field settings, and this may restrict the learning that takes place. Part of establishing an effective service-learning site should be attention to the kind of feedback and opportunities for interaction that students will have. When students are engaged in carrying out focused projects, periodic feedback sessions can be built into the schedule. But it is also sometimes possible to arrange for students to be included in the regular debriefings held by community service organizations to critique events or evaluate programs. Just as real-world service adds an important dimension to the students' learning, engaging in debriefing about authentic lessons learned reinforces the importance of reflection as part of effective practice. For example, college students who were tutoring students in an elementary school occasionally were able to join grade-level teacher teams when they met to discuss plans for students. Students working in an emergency management agency met with staff for incident debriefings.

Reflection After Service

Most service-learning classes require a paper or presentation as an end-of-semester assessment of the service activity. If instructors have attended to the first six cells of the map and students have been engaged in reflection and action throughout the course, then students are in a position to create a more thoughtful final project than if it is their first sustained exploration of the experience.

Creating Activities for Reflection Alone. Final reflective essays in which students are challenged to use their journals as a database and to link their experiences in the field with what they have read and discussed in class are powerful learning tools. Essay projects can take a variety of forms. Students might develop position papers on policies affecting the community. They might discuss a theory introduced in the course, drawing from their experience to illustrate the power of that theory to help explain social phenomena. For example, students in a communication class applied different communication theories to their experiences, making contact with and establishing a project with a community group. One advantage of this exercise was that students were able to make sense of their failures in communication as well as document their triumphs. They might also develop videos, short stories, or other artistic expressions of their experience.

Creating Activities for Reflection with Classmates. When students have been engaged in reflection on their community service throughout the semester, one purpose of postservice activities is to bring a sense of closure to the experience. One approach is to have students or student teams present projects to the class. The projects already identified as suitable for students to undertake alone may also be part of team efforts. For example, students might present policy options in a mock legislative hearing, with their peers questioning and challenging their positions. Some of the roles of those testifying before the hearing might be drawn directly from the community people whom students have worked with during their service. Consider how powerful the testimony of students on welfare reform might be if they could draw on their experiences working with women struggling to cope with the demands of employment and their family situation with limited resources.

Teams might take theories taught during the course and illustrate how they can be applied in understanding community issues or their community project. Service-learning students may also be teamed with students doing more conventional research and create presentations that draw from both forms of inquiry. For example, a powerful presentation on homelessness might include from the work of the service-learners statistical data, historical analysis of the impact of changes in policy from library research, information about how the community currently provides or does not provide needed service, and examples of individuals who are coping with these systems. Community members might be included in the team presentation.

Another approach is to use artistic expression to pull together the threads of the course and the service experience. Students can create a mural during a final class session, explaining the importance of the symbols they add to it, or construct a collage or sculpture that represents the meaning of their experience. One team of students made a video from snapshots they had taken of their project, creating a narrative about their experiences and what they had learned from them.

Creating Activities for Reflection with Community Partners. Part of the value of service-learning is that students are performing a genuine service for the community. There are few more powerful experiences for students than presenting a project they have developed for a community group to representatives of that group and then fielding questions about it. This is particularly meaningful for students when the original project was planned with those in the community to meet needs they identified. An evaluation plan, a grant proposal, a newsletter, and a community needs assessment are examples of projects that students may share with the community.

Conclusion

Reflection is central to effective service-learning. Helping students question their assumptions, identify questions that arise from their experience, or link what they are learning in the classroom with the lives of communities is a continuing challenge. Using the reflection map to guide course planning will ensure that the reflective process in the classroom is effective.

References

Conrad, D., and Hedin, D. *Executive Summary of the Final Report of the Experiential Education Evaluation Project*. Minneapolis: Center for Youth Development and Research, University of Minnesota, 1980.

Eyler, J., and Giles, D. E., Jr. *Where's the Learning in Service-Learning?* San Francisco: Jossey-Bass, 1999.

Eyler, J., Giles, D. E., Jr., and Gray, C. *At a Glance: Summary and Annotated Bibliography of Recent Service-Learning Research in Higher Education*. Minneapolis, Minn.: Learn and Serve America National Service-Learning Clearinghouse, 1999.

Eyler, J., Giles, D. E., Jr., and Schmiede, A. *A Practitioner's Guide to Reflection in Service-Learning: Student Voices and Reflections*. Nashville, Tenn.: Corporation for National Service, 1996.

Honnet, E. P., and Poulsen, S. *Principles of Good Practice in Combining Service and Learning*. Racine, Wis.: Johnson Foundation, 1989.

Kolb, D. *Experiential Learning: Experience as the Source of Learning and Development*. Upper Saddle River, N.J.: Prentice Hall, 1984.

McKnight, J., and Kretzman, J. "Mapping Community Capacity." In M. Minkler (ed.), *Community Organizing and Community Building for Health*. New Brunswick, N.J.: Rutgers University Press, 1997.

Mintz, S. D., and Hesser, G. "Principles of Good Practice in Service-Learning." In B. Jacoby (ed.), *Service-Learning in Higher Education: Concepts and Practices*. San Francisco: Jossey-Bass, 1997.

Moore, D. T. "Behind the Wizard's Curtain: A Challenge to the True Believer." *NSEE Quarterly*, 1999, 25, 23–27.

Sigmon, R. "The Problem of Definition in Service-Learning." In R. Sigmon and Associates, *The Journey to Service-Learning*. Washington, D.C.: Council of Independent Colleges, 1996.

JANET EYLER, associate professor of the practice of education at Vanderbilt University, teaches service-learning courses. She received the National Society for Experiential Education's Outstanding Research Award in 1998.

5

*As an inexpensive, relatively simple means
for sharing information with the community,
the Internet offers new possibilities for
service-learning.*

The Internet in Service-Learning

Mark Canada

With so much work to be done, humans ought to make the most of their energy. Yet every year, millions of young people spend millions of hours on products that go into file cabinets or, worse, wastebaskets. Those young people are American college students, and although their products—assignments they write for school—ideally help them to sharpen their writing and thinking skills, they do little to benefit anyone else. Indeed, unlike their teachers, who often publish the results of their research or use their expertise to advise organizations, most college students write only to learn. Imagine the additional benefits if all of that work lived a life outside the classroom, serving people in need of such information.

Teachers and students who have practiced service-learning do not have to imagine such benefits; they have seen them. By combining course projects with the work of community agencies, they have seen their work benefit not only themselves but social workers, people living with acquired immunodeficiency syndrome (AIDS), and many other members of their communities. Now the Internet has made it easier for faculty and students to share their work with these communities. It makes information exchange easy and inexpensive and enables virtually any class to turn its learning into service-learning.

Two of the many possibilities for using the Internet in service-learning stand out. In one approach, students write and design World Wide Web pages for community agencies, filling these agencies' needs for home pages, press releases, and other material. A more ambitious approach is to create a large Internet clearinghouse of information that both agencies and clients can use. Both approaches promise substantial benefits for communities and students.

NEW DIRECTIONS FOR HIGHER EDUCATION, no. 114, Summer 2001 © John Wiley & Sons, Inc.

Contributing Material to an Agency Web Site

Methods for obtaining information have changed dramatically. Just a few years ago, when we wanted details about an agency or a program, we made a telephone call or picked up a brochure. An 800 number was the zenith of agency-client communication systems. Now we expect every major company, nonprofit organization, college, and government agency to have a World Wide Web site with an overview of its programs, a link to an e-mail address, and perhaps even on-line application forms and other information. An organization without such on-line resources can fully expect to be labeled out-of-date, inefficient, or—perhaps the worst insult of all in these times—not user friendly.

As any organization that has gone on-line can testify, however, the cost of providing such resources can be immense. Writing descriptions, designing interfaces, and converting existing print materials to electronic formats require time and expertise, though surprisingly little money, making them perfect candidates for the help of colleges.

Teachers and students in any discipline can offer this kind of assistance. Obvious providers include classes in content areas such as social work and health. Students in a nutrition class, for example, might collaborate on a glossary of vitamins and minerals to be posted on a health agency's page. But students in skills courses can do this type of service-learning as well. What better people to design an agency's home page, for example, than the students in a computer science class? Composition students learn how to write by writing. Why not assign them essays that convey an agency's mission, programs, or clients to the community? Indeed, Ogburn and Wallace (1998) have described exactly such an assignment that they have used for first-year composition students at the University of Cincinnati.

Once you have decided to use the Internet to do service-learning, you should begin in the same way you would begin many other service-learning projects: contact a partner in the community—in this case, an agency with no Web site or a Web site that needs attention. Finding such an organization should not be difficult. Because of the demands for information, especially new information, even agencies with large, sophisticated sites probably can use help maintaining their on-line calendar, updating their staff directory, or writing descriptions of new programs.

Once you have found an agency interested in collaborating with your students on some Web pages, you will need to discuss exactly what the agency needs. An organization new to the Web will need a home page featuring a summary of its purpose and links to other pages with additional information. Of course, it also will need these other pages, which should include a brief description of each programs it sponsors, some details about the staff, and a link to an e-mail address where visitors can write for more information. Organizations with existing Web sites probably already have these pages, but they may need additional pages or help maintaining their existing pages. For example, they may have added programs since their Web site was designed, or they may have decided to go on-line with their application forms. Organizations that sponsor community events, such as blood drives or an AIDS Awareness Week, may need help creating a promotional page for their site. One frequently overlooked but essential component of a Web site is a detailed description of the organization's staff and mission, along with references to sponsoring or affiliated organizations. Without such information, many Web users may rightfully doubt the credibility of the site.

Some organizations may need additional assistance. Newcomers to the Web, for example, will need not only material to post but also a place to post it. Someone—the instructor, perhaps, or maybe a group of students—will need to locate a server, a computer that can store the organization's Web site and "serve" it up for Web surfers who wish to gain access to it. Internet service providers such as America Online sometimes offer space on their servers to individuals or organizations; agencies can also store their sites on servers managed by on-line companies such as Geocities (www.geocities.com) and Angelfire (www.angelfire.com). Furthermore, both newcomers and agencies with existing sites may need help promoting their sites. The person responsible for this task can contact Web portals, such as Yahoo! and Excite, using their submission procedures.

The next step is to assign these responsibilities to the students in the class. If the agency's needs are diverse, you will want to divide the tasks evenly. For example, if the agency needs both new pages and revisions, each student might update one page and write another. In completing their assignments, students will have to stretch themselves in a number of productive ways as they conduct research, interview agency staff, and then write, design, and post their pages. They probably will need instruction in some areas, particularly those involving technology, and this instruction can be part of the course. Even in a content course, such as one in social work, professors expect students to practice writing in their discipline. In this case, the professor would tailor instruction toward real-life writing for the medium of the Internet. Furthermore, Web-authoring software such as Netscape Composer, which can be downloaded for free from the Web, has made designing and posting Web pages about as easy as writing and printing word processing documents. After giving students a few lessons at the beginning of the semester, professors need only provide guidance throughout the remainder of the course as students write, design, and post their pages.

Building a University-Based Web Resource

A more ambitious approach to using the Internet in service-learning is to build a university-based Web resource that agencies, clients, and indeed anyone else with access to the Internet can use to obtain information about a particular subject. For example, students in an advanced health class might collaborate on a Web site dedicated to promoting exercise and a healthful diet. A business class might produce a Web resource for individuals starting small businesses in the community. This form of service-learning may require more vision and perhaps more work than contributing to an agency's Web site, but it also may bring more satisfaction.

The first step in creating a university-based Web resource is to identify a need. Although the World Wide Web already has millions of sites on a myriad of topics, faculty and students undoubtedly can carve out a niche of their own. If their university is in or near a small community, for example, they can create a site focused on the needs of that community. For instance, a biology class might study the ecology of a city park and report its findings on a Web site. Sites with broader subjects and larger potential audiences may be good projects too. Chances are good, for example, that other people already have used the Web to report on the effects of television violence on children, but the chances are also good that their sites are incomplete, are of dubious credibility, or lack a user-friendly interface. In the end, improving on existing ball-bearing technology is as useful as inventing the wheel.

Like an agency Web site, a university-based Web resource needs a home. Locating a server for such a site should be relatively easy. Faculty should talk to the university's Web administrator about reserving space on the university's server. If possible, obtain a relatively short URL instead of a cumbersome one that tacks a cryptic code onto the university's URL. People in the community will have an easier time dealing with www.cleanwater.edu than with www.uncp.edu/~wilson/bio100/project/water.htm.

The next, and perhaps most stimulating, step is deciding what kind of information will appear on this site. Faculty should involve students in this process, perhaps devoting portions of several class meetings to discussions of contents. Possible components include an overview of the subject, a glossary of terms, a list of links to other relevant and credible Web sites, a link to an e-mail address where users can write for more information, and a collection of frequently asked questions (FAQs) and their answers. For example, a Web resource on healthful living might include general tips on nutrition and exercise, a glossary defining terms such as *vitamin* and *aerobic,* a link to the Web site of the President's Council on Physical Fitness and Sports, and questions and answers about calories, water intake, and sports injuries. As in the case of an agency site, faculty and students should include a section that establishes the site's credibility. In particular, faculty members should identify themselves and their credentials and explain their role in writing and editing the material on the site. Students can divide up the responsibilities for creating and maintaining these components in the same way they would handle the material for an agency site.

Benefits for Communities, Agencies, and Students

Using the Internet for service-learning promises a number of benefits for communities and students. Communities, for example, potentially will enjoy a vast amount of new information to aid in decision making. Indeed, one of the major products of social service agencies is information—about counseling, about treatment, about prevention—and the Internet is an effective medium for exchanging such information. Of course, many potential beneficiaries of this information do not yet have access to the Internet in their homes, but such access may soon become as common as cable television. Furthermore, even those without access at home may be able to log on to the Internet at schools and public libraries.

The agencies serving these communities stand to benefit as well. In exchange for some time devoted to interacting with faculty and students, they will receive a substantial quantity of free public relations material conveniently researched, written, designed, edited, published, and perhaps even maintained by a reputable professor and his or her students. One obstacle that likely keeps many agencies from making optimal use of the Internet is the precious time needed to produce Web pages. Students, however, can commit this time and learn valuable skills and knowledge in the process.

As in the case of other forms of service-learning, students may learn more than they would in a traditional classroom. Simply interacting with social workers and others will provide them with a taste of how these professionals apply their knowledge and skills to address real-life problems and issues. In other words, any type of learning that takes students outside the ivory tower, even briefly and intermittently, teaches the lesson that knowledge is not merely an end in itself. Furthermore, this particular form of service-learning gives students the invaluable opportunity to practice realistic communication with a real audience. Instead of writing a paper—an assignment whose very name suggests a lack of purpose or potency—each student will be contributing to a real project with a real audience. In doing so, he or she will use the same terms—*home page, credibility, mission statement*—and consider the same issues that professionals in the field use. If it is true that writing practice makes better writers, then writing real material with a real purpose in a real context for real audiences can make better real writers—writers who consider the implications of their word choice, strive for accuracy and clarity, perhaps even work passionately because they know that the effectiveness of their product could make a difference for someone in need of help (Bush-Bacelis, 1998).

In an information age, colleges and universities are leading producers of information. Until now, that information—or knowledge, to be more precise—has come almost entirely from professors, who conduct research and then share their findings with colleagues through publication. In the meantime, their students have labored over assigned papers. These messages then took a rather curious, even depressing journey—from the student to the professor to the student and ultimately into a dumpster or a cardboard box stashed in a closet.

The development of the Internet has meant that this student work can go on to live a productive life. With some creativity and planning, faculty can give students real writing experience while at the same time giving their communities information they can use.

References

Bush-Bacelis, J. L. "Innovative Pedagogy: Academic Service-Learning for Business Communication." *Business Communication Quarterly*, 1998, *61*, 20–34.
Ogburn, F., and Wallace, B. "Freshman Composition, the Internet, and Service-Learning." *Michigan Journal of Community Service Learning*, 1998, *5*, 68–74.

MARK CANADA *teaches English at the University of North Carolina at Pembroke and edits the educational Internet site "All American: Literature, History, and Culture" (www.uncp.edu/home/canada/work/allam/allam.htm).*

6

A comprehensive assessment model can measure the effects of service-learning on everyone involved.

A Comprehensive Model for Assessing Service-Learning and Community-University Partnerships

Barbara A. Holland

A Service-Learning Partnership Story

Professor Jane and the city water department strike up a partnership around a federal grant to the city to measure the quality of urban watersheds and develop citizen education programs. Jane wants to expand on her own earlier research on the impact of lawn chemical runoff on watersheds. The city wants to develop plans for improving water quality by assessing current conditions and empowering residents to monitor and minimize their own impacts on water.

Jane prepares her biology class by orienting them to indicators of water quality, as well as urban water issues and policies. The students are trained and supervised by city staff in techniques for collecting water samples in the field. Back in the lab, the students learn methods for analyzing samples, interpret their findings, and write a scientific report for the city. They then practice communication skills by working with neighborhood associations to present their findings, lead field trips, and teach residents about the impact of their domestic actions on water quality. Residents tell students about their neighborhood concerns and in exchange learn how to monitor their local watershed and learn what actions to take if changes occur. The

I acknowledge with deep gratitude the many faculty, staff, students, and community partners who have contributed to this assessment strategy and continue to demonstrate commitment to civic engagement.

students decide to volunteer for a door-to-door campaign to promote detaching home downspouts from sewers to reduce storm flooding.

Jane uses the field data to prepare a research paper on the impact of residential runoff. The city uses the data to develop a strategic plan for water improvement and to review public policies.

Reflection Questions
What are the outcomes of this activity?
Who is responsible for the outcomes?
Who benefited from this service-learning project?
Is this teaching, research, or service?

The answers to the reflection questions seem obvious. A well-designed service-learning activity involves and benefits all participants and requires shared responsibility for planning and outcomes. Service-learning can have multiple and diverse objectives for the same activity: building social responsibility and citizenship skills in students, enhancing student learning through practical experiences, creating synergy between the teaching and research roles of a faculty member, addressing unmet community needs, and increasing community capacity through shared action.

The work of service-learning is complex and multidimensional; it depends on a community-university collaboration in which all parties identify shared goals but also have distinct perspectives. Yet all too often, assessment of service-learning courses is limited to documenting hours of service or collecting journals; worse, it does not happen at all.

As more institutions create service-learning opportunities for students, the links between assessment, effectiveness, and these efforts become clear. However, assessment of such a complex activity can seem daunting. Thus, I suggest a comprehensive assessment model as a method for capturing the different perceptions of and impacts on each constituency participating in service-learning projects and for promoting ongoing improvement of service-learning programs and the partner relationships that sustain them.

The Role of Partnerships in Assessing Service-Learning

In service-learning settings, students are expected to provide direct community service as part of a course, to learn about and reflect on the community context in which service is provided, and to understand the connection between the service activity and the learning objectives of their course (Driscoll and others, 1998). Service-learning courses require many ingredients: faculty time and expertise, coordination and planning, transportation, community time and expertise, student time and commitment, and resources to fund supplies, materials, and products, to name a few.

The complexity of service-learning results in two major impacts on assessment strategies. First, given limitations of organizational time and resources, an investment in service-learning must be measured for its impact and effectiveness in serving the educational mission of the institution. The return on the effort must justify the investment. This internal, more academic purpose for assessment is also essential to sustaining institutional commitment or expanding faculty involvement in service-learning courses. Faculty want to see evidence that service-learning is making a difference in the learning of course material, student development of social responsibility, or community conditions (Holland, 1999).

Second, an assessment of service-learning that focuses only on students will not capture essential data on the impacts of service-learning on faculty, community partners, and the institution. A service-learning course may meet objectives for student learning, but faculty must also monitor the intense impacts on other participants to improve and sustain the working relationship that is the underpinning of successful service-learning experiences. For service-learning to be sustained, the institution, faculty, students, and community partners must see benefits of shared effort.

Each of these constituents holds different goals and expectations for the project; arrives with different experiences, assets, and fears; and operates from a different sense of power and control. Overcoming differences requires the cultivation of a partnership based on knowledge exchange. Research on the characteristics of partnerships reveals that commitment to assessment activities can help the disparate members of a partnership track their progress and learn from the experience of working together. Assessment tends to put all partners on equal ground by attending to the participation, satisfaction, and perspectives of each stakeholder group (Holland and Ramaley, 1998).

A comprehensive assessment design, introduced at the earliest stages of a collaborative endeavor, such as service-learning, not only measures the impacts of the learning activity, but helps to enrich and sustain the underlying partnership itself. Yet assessment and evaluation often receive short shrift in the planning of most grants, projects, courses, and new programs. Many faculty are not assessment experts and avoid issues of assessment and evaluation unless program guidelines or administrative direction require that they consider them. However, as new initiatives in higher education, service-learning programs and community-university partnerships depend on effective assessment strategies to generate the evidence that will sustain internal and external support and document impacts. In addition, effective assessment can ensure consistent quality of effort and experience, build the body of knowledge about best practices, develop the evidentiary argument for additional resources, motivate others to participate by documenting outcomes, and generate ideas and lessons learned to share with others.

Assessment can also identify problem areas where improvement is needed, illuminate key issues and challenges, compare and contrast strategies and actions, and document successes that warrant celebration. In addition, new work as complex as service-learning inspires us to wonder about the outcomes. Have you ever thought, "I wonder if this experience made a difference for the students or community members" or "That activity didn't seem to go the way I thought it would. I wonder what should be changed for next time." Answering these questions means planning ahead for the assessment of new activities even though you may not know all the questions before you begin—which is another reason to take a comprehensive approach.

Before you begin to design an assessment, consider using the following questions for individual or group reflection (Holland, Gelmon, and Baker, 1998; Shinnamon, Gelmon, and Holland, 1999; Gelmon, 2000).

- What is the purpose of my assessment?
- Who wants or needs the assessment information?
- What resources are available to support assessment?
- Who will conduct the assessment?
- How can I ensure the results are used?

The assessment of service-learning courses should begin by considering the balance between the curiosity that inspires us to question why things happen or how to make something better and the reality of the effort it takes to gain such understanding. These planning questions help ensure that the scope and scale of your assessment plan align with your objectives, resources, and audience. Engaging all constituents in exploring these questions also helps build trust and a greater awareness of common and different interests in the partnership.

Origins and Design of the Comprehensive Assessment Model

The issue of multiple goals and multiple constituencies is a major challenge to the task of evaluating service-learning. In addition, a common problem with assessment is the misguided collection of massive amounts of data without a clear vision of the key questions or an analytical framework to create a way of understanding what the data reveal. The model described here offers a strategy for focusing and organizing the data collection, analysis, and reporting of assessment endeavors where there are multiple goals and perspectives. This comprehensive model distills program or course goals into specific key variables or concepts and then develops one or more measurable indicators for each variable. These measurable indicators are incorporated into a diverse array of qualitative and quantitative methods. A matrix design ensures that every variable and indicator is addressed and that each instrument's contents can be connected back to the goals of the assessment.

The development of this model began with the work of a team of faculty, students, and community members from Portland State University (PSU) who created a case study method for analyzing the impacts of service-learning on faculty, students, community, and institution (Driscoll and others, 1998). This approach focuses on capturing and interpreting the impacts that each constituency experiences. Rather than attempting to look only at general effects, this model uses specific measures of impacts and distinctive instruments for each group.

In this way, the assessment captures information that characterizes changes in the capacities, attitudes, and perceptions of participants, as well as their own subjective and objective perceptions of the value and effectiveness of the experience. Measuring those changes or impacts provides information that can be directly applied to improving the performance of service-learning activities as the partnership goes forward, new projects are initiated, or new community partners are added. Also, the design process provides a sharply focused guide for data collection and analysis, thus ensuring a systematic and structured interpretation of the information in a manner that increases the validity and reliability of findings (Strauss and Corbin, 1990).

Originally the PSU model was developed and piloted as a method for assessing the impacts of service-learning as a central component of PSU's sweeping reform of general education. This assessment framework has since been used by many other institutions to assess the impacts of service-learning or other types of civic engagement activities involving partnerships and multiple constituencies. One example is a national grant project to promote service-learning in health professions education: the Health Professions Schools in Service to the Nation (HPSISN) program involving nineteen institutions of all types (Gelmon, Holland, and Shinnamon, 1998). The HPSISN adaptation is a useful example of shaping variables and indicators to reflect unique goals relevant to certain service-learning contexts and courses—in this case, the health professions.

The Assessment Framework. The comprehensive model for assessing service-learning is based on a goal-variable-indicator-method design:

- Goal: What do we want to know?
- Variable: What will we look for?
- Indicator: What will be measured?
- Method: How will it be measured?

This approach to assessment of service-learning begins with an exploration of goals and objectives. The question to ask is, "What do we want to know?" For example, a broad goal may be to increase the sense of social responsibility in students, and the hypothesis may be that service-learning will have a positive impact on students' attitudes and actions as citizens.

The next step is to break a large goal into specific areas of interest by asking, "What will we look for to find evidence of the impact of service-learning?" The task is to identify key issues that can be characterized as major variables of your assessment. Examples of key variables or concepts you might derive from the goal on social responsibility (depending on your students' characteristics and other learning goals you have for them) include

- Awareness of community issues
- Involvement with community
- Concern about career goals and other interests
- Commitment to service

For each of these variables, the question to ask to generate measurable indicators as evidence of the presence or absence of progress toward the variable and its larger goal is, "What will be measured?" For the variable for commitment to service, indicators might include

- Hours of participation
- Level of participation over time
- Reactions to the challenges of service
- Intentions regarding future service

The final question, "How will it be measured?" guides the selection and design of methods for data collection. The questions in every instrument and protocol are linked to specific indicators to ensure that every indicator is measured (usually in more than one way) and that every data element collected has a purpose, thus facilitating analysis. Multiple indicators of each variable and multiple methods for measuring each indicator contribute to validity. In the example, the indicators might be measured using the following strategies:

- Hours of participation: survey, observation, logs
- Level of participation over time: survey, interview, observation
- Reactions to the challenges of service: survey, interview, focus group, journals
- Intentions regarding future service: survey, interview, focus group, journals

Using all these methods—or others you might devise—would be very labor intensive, so you will probably want to make some choices. However, this model's strength and record of success and adaptability depend in great part on a commitment to the use of multiple methods for most indicators, in order to cross-check answers and develop a rich understanding of the subjects' attitudes and perceptions. Each method helps to clarify, explain, verify, or elaborate on the data generated by a different method. Each instrument is designed to gather data on a variety of indicators, thus contributing to greater efficiency of effort.

Table 6.1 compares the strengths of different data collection strategies. For each strategy, cells in the matrix are checked to indicate its strengths or

Table 6.1. Comparative Strengths of Assessment Instruments

Instrument	Ease of Data Collection	Ease of Data Analysis	Richness of Data (descriptive)	Flexibility— Open to Unanticipated Data Findings	Promotes Reflection
Survey	x	x			
Interview			x	x	x
Focus groups			x	x	x
Observations			x	x	
Vita analysis	x	x			
Syllabus analysis	x	x			
Journals			x	x	x

Source: Driscoll and others, 1998, p. 17.

advantages. In addition to commonly used tools such as surveys, interviews, and focus groups, the table reports on the strengths of less common strategies that have been useful in service-learning evaluations, especially for capturing change over time or providing another test to corroborate findings from more traditional methods. These other useful strategies include direct observation of service-learning activities, analysis of service-learning course syllabi, analysis of faculty vitae, and analysis of reflection journals of students, faculty, or community partners.

Table 6.1 is useful in comparing the effort required for administration and analysis with the variety and richness of data collected. The best designs seek a balance among dimensions of effort, data quality, and fit with the indicators to be measured.

Instruments. The example given relates to the assessment of impact on students. The identical process of planning can be used to develop variables, indicators, and methods related to goals of the service-learning activity that relate to faculty, community, and the institution. This model is unique in its attention to the perspectives of community partners. Community organizations strive both to contribute to student learning through service and to use the partnership to enhance their own goals and capacity. Following are some examples of the kinds of variables and indicators that might be used to capture community partner impacts:

- Capacity to fulfill mission (new insights into organizational operations, new services initiated, increased capacity to serve clients)
- Economic impacts (value of service-learning services, new or leveraged funding, reduced or increased costs associated with service-learning activity)
- Perception of mutuality and reciprocity (self-articulation of role in project, articulation of goals for the partnership, articulation of benefits to the campus and students, articulation of unanticipated benefits to organization)

- Awareness of potential (analysis of mission or vision, development of new networks of partners, interest in new endeavors)
- Sustainability of partnership (articulation of criteria for success, cost-benefit analysis, perceptions of trust, suggestions for change or improvement)
- Satisfaction (intentions to continue, ability to articulate positive and negative feedback, recruitment of students for continued service or employment, references to service-learning in fundraising or publications, ideas for further interaction)

Engaging Stakeholders in Assessment. The translation of goals and objectives into a set of specific variables whose impact can be measured for each participant group requires consultation with those constituents in the design phase. The process of describing the project, activities, and variables takes time, but it can help ensure that the measurable indicators are an accurate reflection of participants' goals and expectations. Given that the framework attends to both impacts on participants and continuous improvement of the activity, the indicators chosen usually include a combination of measures of specific outcomes as well as attitudes, perceptions, and processes that are inherent to service-learning endeavors. Both process and product matter.

This shared approach to designing assessment especially helps community participants acquire a shared vocabulary, expand their understanding of the learning objectives of the project for students, and thus create a greater sense of common purpose. Again, we see that the processes of assessment design and implementation are tools for enhancing collaboration, trust, and reciprocity in the partnership that supports service-learning.

Challenges and Pitfalls of Assessment. Many pitfalls are associated with assessment, and most can be attributed to a lack of advance articulation of purpose, audience, resources, and dissemination strategies. The model proposed in this chapter compels designers to give early attention to planning as a means of avoiding most of the common problems with assessment design, implementation, and analysis. However, all assessments are challenging, and it is useful to be aware of the key issues that can trip up good work.

Without question, a comprehensive and ongoing assessment strategy requires substantial investment and commitment. The advantages conferred by such a plan (short- and long-term findings, greater trust among partners, information for continuous improvement) must be balanced with a realistic view of the time, expense, and human effort involved in assessment. Those participating in planning assessment programs will need to consider operational and practical issues to create a plan that has the potential to be fully implemented and sustained.

A comprehensive assessment plan generates a large amount of raw data that must be reviewed, analyzed, and gathered into appropriate reporting formats. Too often, idealistic assessment plans stall after one round, are reduced in scope, or never begin at all because the design was not specific in delineating responsibilities, timetables, and a strategy for analysis and reporting.

An assessment plan must be of a scale in keeping with available resources—human, technical, and financial. What parts of the plan will be accomplished by an individual, a campus unit, a partnership committee? Where does ultimate leadership reside? The plan should clearly assign responsibilities for the assessment tasks of design, data collection, analysis, writing, and dissemination, including the development of an implementation budget.

Assessment design should also consider the availability of expertise. The instruments and analytical methods of assessment require specific skills and training. The temptation to say, "Let's make up a survey," belies the sophistication necessary for assessment tasks. Conducting assessments without the support of requisite design and analysis skills can lead to findings that have little meaning or impact on the program. Stakeholders and decision makers who will consider the results of assessment will be influenced by the quality of data and the synthesis. Individuals or institutions with limited access to internal expertise may want to adopt strategies, instruments, or protocols developed by other institutions or seek the advice of experts from other programs.

Conclusion

Too often we are tempted to undertake a new endeavor such as service-learning without sufficient attention to planning for assessment of the new activity. Or we wait until the end and then look at summative outcomes, which means we cannot really explain what contributed to or limited the outcomes we see. In addition, the growing commitment to service-learning is compelling institutions to make significant changes in academic work and culture. To extend and sustain these changes requires documenting the impact of service-learning and the effectiveness of strategies and methods of organizing the partnerships that sustain service-learning.

This model's strength is its attention to the complex dynamics behind service-learning—the collaborative work of students, faculty, their institutional context, and their community partners. By gathering systematic feedback from each group, the assessment strategy ensures that the entire service-learning endeavor is documented and improved. The design requires great effort in the beginning—to reach agreement on goals and develop appropriate variables, indicators, and methods—so that analysis can be done efficiently and accurately and can lead to compelling findings.

Expansion of service-learning into a broader array of courses, disciplines, and institutions will depend to a great degree on the ability of the first wave of service-learning faculty and campus leaders, the pioneers, to document and assess the work and the outcomes of service-learning. Many of those who follow will be persuaded by the strong evidence of impacts captured through a formal and systematic strategy of assessment. In addition, the inclusive nature of this assessment model, especially the equal attention to community impacts and perspectives, is consistent with the collaborative values of service-learning, citizenship, and partnership.

References

Driscoll, A., Gelmon, S., Holland, B., Kerrigan, S., Spring, A., Grosvold, K., and Longley, M. *Assessing the Impact of Service Learning: A Workbook of Strategies and Methods.* (2nd ed.) Portland, Oreg.: Center for Academic Excellence, Portland State University, 1998.

Gelmon, S. B. "How Do We Know That Our Work Makes a Difference? Assessment Strategies for Service-Learning and Civic Engagement." *Metropolitan Universities,* 2000, *11,* 28–39.

Gelmon, S. B., Holland, B. A., and Shinnamon, A. F. *Health Professions Schools in Service to the Nation 1996–98. Final Evaluation Report.* San Francisco: Community-Campus Partnerships for Health, Center for the Health Professions, University of California at San Francisco, 1998.

Holland, B. A. "Factors and Strategies That Influence Faculty Involvement in Public Service." *Journal of Public Service and Outreach,* 1999, *4,* 37–43.

Holland, B. A., Gelmon, S. B., and Baker, G. R. "Involving Stakeholders in Forming Good Assessment Questions for Continuous Improvement." Paper presented at the Conference on Assessment and Quality, American Association for Higher Education, Cincinnati, Ohio, 1998.

Holland, B. A., and Ramaley, J. A. "What Partnership Models Work to Link Education and Community Building? How Do We Know?" Paper presented at Connecting Community Building and Education Reform: Effective School, Community, University Partnerships, a Joint Forum of the U.S. Department of Education and U.S. Department of Housing and Urban Development, Washington, D.C., Jan. 1998.

Shinnamon, A., Gelmon, S. B., and Holland, B. A. *Methods and Strategies for Assessing Service-Learning in the Health Professions.* San Francisco: Community-Campus Partnerships for Health, Center for the Health Professions, University of California at San Francisco, 1999.

Strauss, A., and Corbin, J. *Basics of Qualitative Research: Grounded Theory Procedures and Techniques.* Thousand Oaks, Calif.: Sage, 1990.

BARBARA A. HOLLAND *is a senior scholar at Indiana University–Purdue University Indianapolis. During 2000–2001, she directed the Office of University Partnerships at the U.S. Department of Housing and Urban Development.*

7

Organizations such as the National Society for Experiential Education provide educators with support for improving service-learning initiatives.

The National Society for Experiential Education in Service-Learning

Lawrence Neil Bailis

Service-learning has been an integral part of the broader movement to promote learning through experience for decades, long before anyone used the term *service-learning*. Indeed, promotion of service-learning, along with internships and other forms of experiential learning, has been central to the National Society for Experiential Education (NSEE) since its founding nearly thirty years ago. The NSEE advocates the use of all forms of experiential learning in the education system and the community, enhancing the professional growth of members, disseminating information on principles of good practice, and encouraging the development and dissemination of research related to experiential learning.

A Contact Point for Experts and Peers

The NSEE serves teachers, community leaders, and others interested in service-learning first by putting them in touch with top thinkers in the field. Through a resource center, the NSEE Annual Conference, regional meetings, the *NSEE Quarterly,* and a range of NSEE publications, educators and others can explore the latest developments in service-learning, such as emerging quality standards. While educators can tap other national resources for expertise on service-learning, NSEE's broad focus on experiential education allows them to draw on ideas from related fields such as internships and work-based learning. Taken together, NSEE resources enable people to obtain education, training, and professional development in the foundations of service-learning and related experiential education

The author would like to thank Donna Sizemore Hale for her contributions to this chapter.

fields, in specialized topics such as using older students to mentor younger ones, and in particular functions such as building partnerships or reflection. Educators can find additional information about the expertise available from NSEE on its World Wide Web site (www.nsee.org).

Many of these mechanisms also provide opportunities for teachers and community leaders to exchange ideas with peers across the country. In addition to its annual conference and regional meetings, the NSEE is working on a number of electronic resources that facilitate communication among members. Web-searchable on-line membership lists, for example, allow NSEE members to contact other members with identified interests and expertise. Furthermore, members will have access to a variety of chat rooms where they can discuss already identified topics on an ongoing basis or propose new topics for discussion.

A Generator and Incubator of New Approaches

Despite—or perhaps because of—its long association with service-learning, NSEE leaders and many of its members began to see some inherent limits in the organization's efforts to support service-learning in the early 1990s. In particular, the episodic nature of the links between educators and community leaders meant that an inordinate amount of time and energy had to be spent on the processes of linking schools and communities, thereby limiting the time that could be devoted to improving program quality. Educators who were new to service-learning had to find ways to identify community partners and then begin to work with them. Those who already had worked with the community typically had to start anew at the beginning of each school year or semester if they wanted to keep the service-learning momentum going.

As a result of numerous discussions about these kinds of realizations, NSEE leaders began to work with members to develop a new service-learning model in which educators and community leaders would form sustainable partnerships transcending specific projects. The new approach allows for years-long development of mutual understanding and extended planning periods that permit service-learning to achieve its full potential, providing quality experiential learning opportunities to students while meeting real community needs.

Using Sustainable Partnerships

During the early 1990s, NSEE members typically brought two broad perspectives to the numerous sessions on service-learning at the annual conferences. The first stressed the power of the approach and the benefits that accrue to the participants. The second addressed the barriers these participants faced in designing and implementing quality service-learning experiences. The challenge was clear: to maximize the former and minimize the latter.

From the educators' perspective, the problems were exacerbated by the constant need to start fresh—to identify new community partners, understand their needs, make sure they understand the benefits that can accrue to using students who are completing course work as resources in their agencies, and then work with them and the students to develop meaningful service experiences. Once a project was completed, educators had to start all over again with a new set of community actors.

As a result of ongoing interactions with the membership, NSEE began to explore ways to overcome this obstacle. Although the term *sustainable partnerships* was not used until several years later, the idea became clear. If it were possible to create partnerships that would last over years, the educators and community partners would get to know each other better, resulting in numerous tangible and intangible benefits. In particular, these partnerships would improve the quality of their joint efforts by making it possible to devise projects that were better attuned to the needs of all partner agencies, drawing on input from educators, community agency staff, and the students themselves. In addition, this kind of arrangement would minimize the start-up costs of service-learning by reducing or eliminating the time it takes educators to identify appropriate community partners and then to work with them to develop appropriate service-related activities for students. Perhaps most important, the periodic meetings among educators and community partners allow an opportunity for meaningful student input into the earliest stages of project planning.

The National Community Development Program

NSEE was ideally positioned to put this idea into action. NSEE staff began planning for the National Community Development Program (NCDP) in early 1996, exploring program models and potential funders. In 1997, funding from the Surdna and Ford foundations made it possible to announce the selection of partnership teams from Gettysburg, Pennsylvania; San Diego, California; and Durham, North Carolina. All three communities included educators who had been involved with NSEE. The participating partners and objectives of the three teams are summarized in Table 7.1.

NCDP operations were closely integrated into ongoing NSEE activities. NSEE staff visited the sites to help get the planning under way and to find concrete ways for creating ongoing partnership activities. The staff served simultaneously as sounding board, prod, and monitor. Furthermore, the partners at each site were offered the support of a peer facilitator who would be hired by NSEE to provide feedback and otherwise support the process of planning and running partnerships. In each case, the facilitators were active NSEE members who worked in close contact with the NSEE staff who had set the demonstration effort in motion.

The partners from each of the three teams were brought together at the annual NSEE conferences to share information and participate in the

Table 7.1. Overview of the NCDP Community Partnerships

	College Partner		
	Durham: North Carolina Central University	Gettysburg, Pa.: Gettysburg College	San Diego, Calif.: University of San Diego
High school partners	Hillside High School	Gettysburg High School Lincoln Intermediate Unit #12 migrant program	Mark Twain Junior and Senior High School
Community partners	Durham County Health Department Operation Breakthrough (community action agency)	South Central Community Action Program	San Diego Parks and Recreation Department Social Advocates for Youth (San Diego)
Initial planned focus	Health education issues, especially lead paint	Literacy	Youth development and the environment
Current focus	Health education issues	Cultural awareness and respect for diversity	Youth development and the environment

broader range of NSEE professional development opportunities. These opportunities to interact more closely with each other and with their colleagues in other communities resulted in a range of benefits, including an off-site retreat where they could get to know each other better and begin to work more closely together than would have been possible in regular monthly meetings. The opportunities also allowed partners to meet their counterparts from other communities and to learn to put their own experiences in context—coming to see, for instance, that others had been facing the same challenges. Finally, they put the partners in touch with leading educators in the field. In one instance, this exposure led to a total revamping of the goals and approaches taken by the community partnership.

Formal support for the three communities ended in the fall of 2000, but NSEE has continued to stay in contact with the three of them and to provide assistance, including limited support for a few partners to continue attending NSEE annual conferences.

Several interim reports have made it clear that the idea of sustainable partnerships makes sense, that NSEE has been effective in turning this idea into a reality at three sites, and that the partnerships have indeed been sustaining themselves and are producing solid benefits. For example, a January 2000 report concluded that the community partnerships in Durham, Gettysburg, and San Diego have all remained active, sustained themselves, and grown in terms of numbers of partners and quality of interaction (Bailis, 2000). In each case, the K-12, college, and community partners have continued to meet monthly. In each case, either the same staff have remained active throughout or replacements have been named and joined in from the same agencies. There is a growing student voice in at least two of them, which has led to growth in both the quantity and quality of service-learning at all three sites. In all cases, the partnerships have moved beyond functional bodies that support activities to the point where members are making close personal relationships and providing emotional support for each other. Knowing more about other partners is, in their opinion, the key to being able to tailor service offerings. In short, the NCDP track record shows that the process of promoting and sustaining partnerships can be productively supported from the outside with a relatively modest investment of resources.

Conclusion

NSEE has documented decades of efforts to bring community people into classrooms and classroom students into the community. It has accumulated a wide range of experience and expertise on such basic issues as integrating service into academic curricula, finding meaningful ways to enable students to reflect on their experiences, and moving from the concept of the community as a site for service to the community as a sustained partner of educational institutions. The challenge is moving abstract ideas to practical vehicles that educators can adopt without the resources and attention characteristic of foundation-supported demonstration projects. NSEE has made this happen in the past, and it stands ready to make it happen in the future.

Reference

Bailis, L. N. *Evaluation of the National Community Development Program—Update Report.* Alexandria, Va.: National Society for Experiential Education, 2000.

LAWRENCE NEIL BAILIS, *associate research professor at Brandeis University's Heller Graduate School, leads the independent third-party evaluation of the NSEE demonstration program described in this chapter.*

*Three strategies for overcoming the challenges
of advancing and institutionalizing service-learning
at research universities are offered.*

8

Advancing Service-Learning at Research Universities

Andrew Furco

The pedagogy of service-learning—the integration of community service into the academic curriculum—has been incorporated increasingly into the academic fabric of many colleges and universities around the country. Service-learning is rooted in the theories of constructivism and experiential education. According to a number of experts, service-learning is a teaching strategy that enhances students' learning of academic content by engaging them in authentic activities in which they apply the content of the course to address identified needs in the local and broader community (Bringle and Hatcher, 1995; Howard, 1998). Jacoby and Associates (1996) write, "As a pedagogy, service-learning is education that is grounded in experience as a basis for learning and on the centrality and intentionality of reflection designed to enable learning to occur" (p. 9).

Given that service-learning is cast primarily (although not exclusively) as a pedagogy, it is not surprising that its growth in higher education has been most prominent at the colleges and universities that emphasize teaching, such as liberal arts colleges, comprehensive colleges, and other teaching-focused institutions. At research institutions, however, service-learning activity and institutional support for faculty involvement in service-learning have not been as strong (Rothman, 1998). This is not surprising given that these institutions emphasize research over teaching and therefore are less inclined to have a concerted, campuswide effort to promote the advancement of a particular pedagogy.

This issue brings into question the role of service-learning at research universities. Although teaching is certainly an essential component of research institutions, the production and publication of high-quality research take center stage as the predominant benchmark by which faculty performance is measured (Boyer, 1987). Nevertheless, service-learning is as appropriate for faculty at research universities as it is for faculty at other types of higher education institutions.

The Purposes of Research Institutions

The research university in the United States grew out of German academic traditions and structures that sought to ensure a focus on pure research that was "wholly unconstrained by narrow utilitarian considerations" (Lucas, 1994, p. 171). In his treatise of the history of American higher education, Lucas writes, "Especially impressive to American observers was the Germanic emphasis upon the disinterested pursuit of truth through original scholarly investigation" (p. 172). Throughout the second half of the eighteenth century, many colleges that had disseminated knowledge primarily through teaching were now being transformed to emphasize scholarly research and disseminate knowledge through investigation and publication. In this regard, higher education institutions shifted from being knowledge transmitters to knowledge generators.

The growth of knowledge, the rise of disciplinary specialization, the establishment of empiricism as the hallmark of inquiry in all disciplines, and the influx of federal funds during the first half of the twentieth century gave research universities prominence and esteem. And despite both the growing role of the states in funding and shaping higher education and the rise of the competitive corporate-academe environment in the second half of the century, the status and prominence of research in higher education have not faltered (Lucas, 1994). Today, even institutions that do not classify themselves as a research college or research university consider research productivity and all of the expectations that go along with it—garnering of research grants, scholarly publications, production of new knowledge—to be an essential gauge of the quality and status of their institution. The college and graduate school rankings of *U.S. News and World Report* provide a perfect example of how high in esteem we hold those institutions that make research the primary focus of their work.

Because of the centrality of research, teaching activities at research institutions, albeit necessary, are not what get faculty promoted or advance institutions in their national rankings. And for faculty members at research universities who genuinely enjoy teaching, deciding how much time to devote to teaching and how much time to devote to research can be a source of ongoing tension. The primary rewards for these faculty members are rooted in the level and quality of their research activity, the garnering of research funds, and the production of influential publications. It is highly unlikely that faculty members at research universities who are not successful in one or more of these research-centered activities will be granted tenure, even if they maintain a heavy course load and are excellent teachers (Boyer, 1987).

The existing research-centered expectations and norms can be a disincentive for faculty at research institutions to explore and pursue activities that are perceived to be nonscholarly and nonresearch focused. Such activities might include the exploration of new and innovative teaching practices, the development of community partnerships, the use of new techniques for assessing students, and the production of publications intended for nonacademic audiences. The prevailing institutional norms and expectations are disincentives, especially for junior faculty, whose early career choices and level of productivity will have long-term effects on their careers. Without inducements and incentives for faculty members at research universities to explore various pedagogies, the advancement of service-learning at research universities is likely to remain a slow and difficult process.

The Role of Faculty in Advancing Service-Learning

A University of California–Berkeley study of the process of institutionalizing service-learning at forty-five colleges and universities in the western United States found that the strongest predictor for institutionalizing service-learning on college campuses is faculty involvement in and support for service-learning (Bell and others, 2000). The study, which examined two-year community colleges, four-year private institutions, and four-year public institutions, found that even when institutional rewards and incentives are in place for faculty to participate in service-learning, faculty members agree to expend the time and energy to develop high-quality service-learning experiences for their students only when they are convinced that engaging in service-learning will not be viewed negatively by their peers or the campus administration. This finding was true across all types of institutions.

The Berkeley study found that without the genuine support and involvement of a critical mass of faculty, service-learning is likely not to become institutionalized on a campus to any significant degree (Bell and others, 2000). Therefore, one of the first steps to advancing service-learning on any campus is to develop a critical mass of faculty who support and promote its use.

At institutions where faculty members are rewarded actively for employing effective, innovative teaching strategies that improve student learning, service-learning can be a welcome approach among faculty. At such institutions (examples are Portland State University and California State University–Monterey Bay), faculty members know that their efforts to implement effective pedagogies, such as service-learning, will be perceived by their colleagues and administrators as a valuable part of their teaching scholarship. On these campuses, the institutional culture provides the seedbed out of which a critical mass of faculty supporters for service-learning can sprout and grow.

At institutions where the scholarship of teaching is not the predominant barometer for professional advancement and the prevailing institutional culture does not look favorably on applied learning, faculty members are likely to be more reticent in supporting service-learning as a legitimate academic, scholarly pursuit. Focused on conducting high-quality research within their disciplinary specialty area, faculty members at research institutions must be convinced that service-learning can enhance and advance their roles as researchers and scholars.

Strategies for Advancing Service-Learning

How then does one surmount a research university's prevailing institutional norms and expectations to forge a critical mass of faculty members who genuinely support the advancement of service-learning? Three strategies for advancing service-learning at research universities are offered. First, service-learning must be tied to the scholarly activities that research faculty value most. Second, service-learning must be tied to the important academic goals and initiatives under way on the campus. And third, service-learning must be incorporated strategically into the disciplinary structure of the university. In each case, the goal is to make service-learning a more important component of the academic structures and practices that are valued most at research universities. This goal can be accomplished only through a concerted effort that is led by both the faculty and the campus administration.

Service-Learning and Faculty Research. The best means of garnering support for service-learning from faculty at research universities is to connect service-learning to faculty research work (Bell and others, 2000). For this connection to happen, campus administrators need to promote service-learning as a philosophy rather than as a pedagogy. In many ways, service-learning is not only about teaching; it also involves the theoretical and practical exploration and investigation of social issues through a particular disciplinary lens. Pedagogically, students address the needs of the community through their application of a course's academic content. However, faculty can use the service-learning experiences of their students to engage their own expertise in the research of important community issues.

According to Reardon (1998), an increasing number of colleges and universities are recognizing the scholarly benefits of having faculty incorporate service-learning into their research activities. Many of the civic and social issues that are addressed through service-learning incorporate numerous theories, philosophies, and concepts that are rooted in a variety of disciplines, including economics, sociology, public health, law, business, education, and psychology. Enos and Troppe (1996) suggest that research is an integral part of all service-learning since the solutions to community problems addressed in the service-learning experience should be based on the application of findings derived from research. By aligning one's research interests and disciplinary specialization with a pertinent aspect of the social issue that is being addressed by students in the service-learning course, a faculty member can use service-learning to advance his or her research agenda.

For example, a faculty member in atmospheric sciences whose research work is focused on issues of global warming might engage students in a service-learning project in which they survey various populations about their understanding of global warming and its causes. The survey might pose questions about the everyday practices the subjects employ that potentially contribute to the advancement or reduction of global warming. The students can then use the data gathered from their surveys to develop informational materials that inform the public about the causes and hazards of global warming. Furthermore, the faculty member can use the data to inform his or her own investigations. In this case, the faculty member might use the data to develop a demographic profile of people's awareness of global warming. This profile might be used in identifying a representative sample for a future study.

Some faculty members who are involved in long-term research projects have used service-learning as a means to develop long-term relationships with agencies that can assist them in identifying potential research subjects. By engaging a group of students in various service-learning activities in the same set of agencies over several semesters, faculty members can make these agencies essential partners for identifying research subjects and sites for their own investigations. And for the kinds of research grants that many federal agencies offer, such long-term partnerships can be assets in the funding competition.

One of the concerns about using service-learning for the purposes of research is that it challenges the traditional professional-expert research model (Reardon, 1998). Because successful service-learning experiences are predicated on effective campus-community partnerships, members of the community play an important role in designing and shaping the scope of the research investigation. Often referred to as participatory action research, this form of research is not always highly regarded by pure academicians and basic researchers. However, Reardon (1998), Jacoby and Associates (1996), and others argue that participatory action research is a more effective and meaningful form of research than basic research because its direct relevance to the needs of the community "increases the potential for implementation of recommendations emerging from these research efforts" (Reardon, 1998, p. 59). The results of participatory action research investigations not only make contributions to a body of disciplinary knowledge but also culminate in a set of recommendations that are then implemented through action (Jacoby and Associates, 1996).

A second justification for connecting service-learning activities to faculty research is that faculty members can garner publications, research grants, and public recognition by engaging in community-based research that is facilitated through students' service-learning activities. Using service-learning as a vehicle to investigate social issues that are tied to a faculty member's area of expertise can prove to be a viable and productive means for faculty at research universities (and other types of higher education institutions) to promote and advance their research agendas. Focusing one's research on issues of immediate social importance can help raise the visibility and broaden the appeal of a faculty member's research work. The service-learning work of students can help faculty generate ideas, topics, and designs for research.

Not all courses and not all areas of study lend themselves easily to service-learning, and not all service-learning experiences generate research activity for faculty. Nevertheless, in many instances across the spectrum of academic disciplines, service-learning can be a vehicle for advancing some aspect of a faculty member's research work. As faculty members begin to use service-learning to advance their research agendas, their buy-in for service-learning can be more firmly secured.

Long-term faculty support for service-learning comes only if the campus administration gives legitimacy to community-based research. The Berkeley institutionalization study found that after faculty support for service-learning, institutional support for service-learning was the second strongest predictor for institutionalizing service-learning in higher education (Bell and others, 2000). Specifically, the findings reveal that to advance the service-learning institutionalization process, campus administrators must set up institutional structures and mechanisms that support faculty engagement in service-learning. Unless the institution genuinely recognizes service-learning as a legitimate academic pursuit that enhances faculty scholarship, faculty members, especially junior faculty, will shy away from participating in service-learning over any significant portion of time (Holland, 1999; Ward, 1998).

At research institutions, the support structures and mechanisms to be put in place might include the establishment of an interdisciplinary research center that brings together faculty members who are interested in community-based research. Other structures might include research grant support to faculty members who want to tie their disciplinary research to investigations related to issues in the local community or the formal consideration of service-learning in the campus's promotion, review, and tenure policies. These kinds of structures and mechanisms not only send the message to faculty members that the institution supports their work in service-learning, but also provide a forum for faculty members who use service-learning in various disciplines to come together, share their experiences, and air their concerns. Such campuswide, cross-disciplinary faculty initiatives and incentives are essential for the development of a critical mass of faculty who support service-learning on a campus (Bell and others, 2000).

Service-Learning and the University Mission. The advancement of service-learning at research universities does not reside solely with the faculty. The institution itself must have structures and mechanisms in place that support the service-learning work of faculty. What incentives does the campus administration of a research university have to establish these support structures and mechanisms?

One rationale for establishing structures and mechanisms that support faculty members' work in service-learning is that service-learning can be a vehicle to achieve many of the overarching goals of research institutions. On the surface, the goals of service-learning (such as the application of knowledge to address community needs) seem antithetical to the primary knowledge-generating purposes of research universities. However, over the years, the purely nonutilitarian emphasis of research universities has not existed without debate.

Ironically, the growing emphasis on research in higher education came in the early 1900s, at the start of the Progressive era, which emphasized social and civic service. As higher education institutions were being called on to assist in addressing the social problems of the day, research universities worked to develop formal ties with their local communities. The formation of the land grant institutions was one of the earliest manifestations of this effort. The University of Wisconsin's proclamation that it would focus on tying its research with community needs encouraged other universities around the country to adopt similar stances. It was not long before research institutions such as the University of Michigan, Harvard University, and the University of Chicago were engaging students in their communities to address a variety of social issues (Lucas, 1994).

Although the social and civic purposes of higher education were revisited at several points throughout the twentieth century, these purposes never supplanted the focus on pure research investigation, scholarly publication, and research grant acquisition. Much of the rhetoric surrounding the civic and social purposes of higher education has been rooted in the debate over utilitarian (social, professional) versus liberal (academic) purposes of education. And although attempts have been made over the years to strike a balance between these purposes, the research universities have tended to place emphasis on the more liberal aspects of education (Boyer, 1987).

The pendulum has not ceased to swing. The rise of service-learning in the 1990s was to some degree a reaction to the growing concern that higher education had grown "utterly remote and removed from the vital concerns with which academic inquiry had once been engaged" (Lucas, 1994, p. 287). According to Lucas, the strongest criticism has been against the research universities—ivory towers where the specializations and subspecializations of faculty create environments where serious scholarship is confined to "small problems, narrowly drawn topics and issues, and in-depth analysis of subjects of microscopic proportions and sharply delimited boundaries," which results in research that "does not contribute much of significance to the general populace or any particular segment thereof" (p. 286).

Such criticisms of higher education have recently spawned a series of reform initiatives that have sought to reshape some of the purposes of higher education. These reforms have included efforts to improve the curriculum and teaching of undergraduate education by providing increased focus on the scholarship of teaching, to shed the ivory tower image through the development of campus-community partnerships in which faculty can explore a scholarship of engagement, and to address the potentially limiting focus of disciplinary specialization through the fostering of intellectual cross-disciplinary learning communities. These reforms have begun to gain legitimacy at a number of colleges and universities, including research universities, around the country. Interestingly, many of these reform initiatives are closely aligned with the philosophy, goals, and pedagogy of service-learning.

Since the early 1990s, higher education has taken a critical look at its teaching practices, especially in the area of undergraduate education. The efforts to improve undergraduate education have been strongest at the teaching colleges. For the research universities, which place greater emphasis on graduate education, the focus on improving faculty teaching effectiveness has remained less strong. However, although research productivity remains the predominant factor in the advancement of faculty at research institutions, the late 1990s saw a shift at research universities toward placing greater emphasis on teaching effectiveness.

If the engagement of students in service is an effective pedagogy for improving student learning, as a number of service-learning experts have claimed (Eyler and Giles, 1999), then administrators of research universities might want to consider supporting faculty members' incorporation of service-learning in their courses. The development and implementation of a service-learning course can assist faculty members in demonstrating their scholarship of teaching. By engaging students in a rigorous, powerful, and meaningful service-learning experience, teachers can increase students' understanding of course concepts (Eyler and Giles, 1999), thus providing themselves with greater teaching success, especially with undergraduate students.

Along with meeting institutional goals of improving teaching practices, service-learning can also help to promote recent efforts in higher education to forge stronger connections between the campus and the local community. Because service-learning is predicated on the involvement of faculty, campus-community collaborations inherently become part of the academic fabric of the institution. The infusion of these partnerships into the academic core of the institution can help stabilize and institutionalize what are often viewed as tenuous and short-lived campus-community collaborations.

For research universities, campus-community collaborations should focus on directly engaging the scholarly expertise of faculty members in addressing the pressing needs of the local and greater community. Through service-learning, faculty can lend their expertise to the community through their research, teaching, and service. This type of comprehensive faculty community engagement, most recently referred to as the scholarship of engagement, focuses on using individual faculty members' expertise to contribute to the public welfare and common good (Boyer, 1996; Driscoll and Lynton, 1999; Schomberg and Farmer, 1994). According to Lynton (1995), service-learning is an effective way to foster faculty members' scholarship of engagement. By seeing community engagement as an important part of faculty members' professional service, research institutions can pave the way for more faculty to see a value in applying their academic expertise to address authentic issues in the community.

There has been some significant movement in this area. In 2000, a national review board for the scholarship of engagement was established by Campus Compact and the American Association for Higher Education (AAHE). This review board is an independent body comprising faculty members from throughout the country who conduct peer reviews of individual faculty members' portfolios to assess the faculty members' scholarship of engagement. The establishment of this review board speaks volumes to the growing legitimacy that the scholarship of engagement is garnering across all types of institutions of higher education.

The social issues that are being addressed in service-learning are often complex and require the implementation of strategies that draw on multiple and varied disciplines and perspectives. For example, addressing the issue of the presence of asbestos in local neighborhood schools could require a collaboration of experts from public health, social welfare, economics, law, education, biology, environmental science, and chemistry. If part of the project is to inform parents and the city about the problem, the project could conceivably draw some expertise from the foreign language department (to translate information to non–English speaking parents), public policy, and psychology.

At many higher education institutions around the country, including research universities, the formation of faculty centers, teaching and learning centers, and other campuswide interdisciplinary forums or spaces for faculty to collaborate on joint ventures is on the rise. Service-learning can be an effective means for getting faculty members to work together across programs and departments. Zlotkowski (1999) writes, "By anchoring itself in real-world projects, [service-learning] naturally serves to pull participating faculty members in the direction of functional and conceptual integration" (p. 111).

Campus administrators can use service-learning to help develop cross-disciplinary learning communities. Along with alleviating some of the professional isolation that faculty members often endure at research universities (Boyer, 1987), these learning communities can help change some of the disciplinary-centered norms of the institution and move the research institution toward legitimizing faculty work in applied, socially relevant research, teaching, and service.

Service-learning should not be viewed as a new, additional program. Instead, a campus administration should view and use it as a vehicle to meet the goals of important educational reform initiatives already taking place on the campus. This is an essential component for advancing service-learning at research universities.

Service-Learning and the Disciplines. The third strategy is to make service-learning a central part of the academic work of the disciplines. The predominant association that faculty members have is with their discipline. When service-learning is genuinely valued within a discipline, faculty members within that discipline begin to view service-learning as a legitimate scholarly pursuit (Holland, 1999).

The production of the monograph series produced by the AAHE on service-learning in the disciplines and the growing presence of service-learning workshops at professional disciplinary association conferences have raised awareness of service-learning across a variety of disciplines. Tying service-learning to what faculty members at research institutions already value—peer-reviewed scholarly publication and professional disciplinary conferences—helps raise its academic legitimacy. As service-learning is presented more prominently in various departments and disciplines, faculty members will begin to perceive it as something that their peers value and consequently something of which they should be cognizant.

Unlike many other programs or initiatives that tend to target a particular discipline or set of disciplines, service-learning is universal; it has potential application to every discipline. And although it is not appropriate for every course, it can be and has been connected to the work of faculty in every discipline. The AAHE monograph series and the wide array of service-learning courses being offered at higher education institutions across the country testify to the universality of service-learning.

Service-learning faculty and campus administrators at research universities should find ways to disseminate the key discipline-based service-learning literature resources to appropriate faculty throughout the campus. Discipline-based conferences and events on service-learning (for example, Campus-Community Partnership for Health conferences and Service-Learning in Teacher Education meetings) should be announced on campuses. Campus administrators and department chairs need to make opportunities available for faculty to attend these meetings and learn about service-learning through the various existing discipline-based associations and networks. It is important that at these gatherings, the faculty are able to meet and converse with faculty members in their discipline from other research universities who are engaged in service-learning. The more that service-learning can be tied to the disciplinary work of faculty, the more likely it is that faculty will consider it an important and legitimate part of their work.

Conclusion

Advancing and institutionalizing service-learning at research universities is predicated on the degree to which service-learning is tied to the work of research faculty and the overall mission and purposes of research universities. At research universities, service-learning must be viewed by faculty members as a valued part of their scholarly work, an essential part of the academic mission of the institution, and a valued component in their discipline. The campus administration must not view service-learning as a separate, independent program, but rather should use it as a means to achieve the goals of broader academic reform initiatives taking place on campus. If service-learning is to be fully advanced and institutionalized at research universities, faculty must be made aware of how it is tied directly not only to their teaching and service activities but also to their research.

Most of the issues addressed in this chapter hold true for all types of higher education institutions, but they are especially important for research universities, where service-learning has seen relatively slow growth. Only when a deliberate and strong scholarly value is placed on service-learning can it be aligned with the academic goals, purposes, and structures of research universities.

References

Bell, R., Furco, A., Ammon, M. S., Muller, P., and Sorgen, V. *Institutionalizing Service-Learning in Higher Education: Findings from a Study of the Western Region Campus Compact Consortium.* Berkeley: University of California, 2000.

Boyer, E. L. *College: The Undergraduate Experience in America.* New York: HarperCollins, 1987.

Boyer, E. L. "The Scholarship of Engagement." *Journal of Public Service and Outreach,* 1996, *1,* 11–20.

Bringle, R., and Hatcher, J. "A Service Learning Curriculum for Faculty." *Michigan Journal of Community Service Learning,* 1995, *1,* 112–122.

Driscoll, A., and Lynton, E. A. *Making Outreach Visible.* Washington, D.C.: American Association for Higher Education, 1999.

Enos, S. L., and Troppe, M. L. "Service-Learning in the Curriculum." In B. Jacoby and Associates, *Service-Learning in Higher Education: Concepts and Practices.* San Francisco: Jossey-Bass, 1996.

Eyler, J., and Giles, D. E., Jr. *Where's the Learning in Service-Learning?* San Francisco: Jossey-Bass, 1999.

Holland, B. "Factors and Strategies That Influence Faculty Involvement in Public Service." *Journal of Public Service and Outreach,* 1999, *4,* 37–43.

Howard, J.P.F. "Academic Service Learning: A Counternormative Pedagogy." In R. A. Rhoads and J.P.F. Howard (eds.), *Academic Service Learning: A Pedagogy of Action and Reflection.* New Directions for Teaching and Learning, no. 73. San Francisco: Jossey-Bass, 1998.

Jacoby, B., and Associates. *Service-Learning in Higher Education: Concepts and Practices.* San Francisco: Jossey-Bass, 1996.

Lucas, C. J. *American Higher Education: A History.* New York: St. Martin's Press, 1994.

Lynton, E. A. *Making the Case for Professional Service.* Washington, D.C.: American Association for Higher Education, 1995.

Reardon, K. "Participatory Action Research as Service Learning." In R. A. Rhoads and J.P.F. Howard (eds.), *Academic Service Learning: A Pedagogy of Action and Reflection.* New Directions for Teaching and Learning, no. 73. San Francisco: Jossey-Bass, 1998.

Rothman, M. (ed.). *Service Matters: Engaging Higher Education in the Renewal of America's Communities and American Democracy.* Providence, R.I.: Campus Compact, 1998.

Schomberg, S. F., and Farmer, J. A. "The Evolving Concept of Public Service and Implications for Rewarding Faculty." *Continuing Higher Education Review,* 1994, *58,* 122–140.

Ward, K. "Addressing Academic Culture: Service Learning, Organizations, and Faculty Work." In R. A. Rhoads and J.P.F. Howard (eds.), *Academic Service Learning: A Pedagogy of Action and Reflection.* New Directions for Teaching and Learning, no. 73. San Francisco: Jossey-Bass, 1998.

Zlotkowski, E. "Pedagogy and Engagement." In R. Bringle (ed.), *Colleges and Universities as Citizens.* Needham Heights, Mass.: Allyn & Bacon, 1999.

ANDREW FURCO is director of the Service-Learning Research and Development Center and a member of the faculty in the Graduate School of Education at the University of California, Berkeley.

9

By addressing systemic issues, faculty in teaching institutions can facilitate participation in and support for service-learning among key stakeholders.

How Professors Can Promote Service-Learning in a Teaching Institution

Kathy O'Byrne

A casual observer might make the assumption that infusing service-learning into a teaching institution is about as difficult as finding a book in the library. After all, teaching institutions pride themselves on quality teaching, and service-learning offers faculty and students the opportunity to reflect on teaching and learning in a meaningful way.

Teaching institutions have their own sets of challenges in this regard, however. They are textured, multilayered academic cultures that create complicated and often fragmented challenges for ambitious faculty members. Not the least of these challenges comes with the realization that the finest instructors in the land will not be granted tenure without a record of scholarship. Most universities also expect that faculty will engage in service, alternately defined by service to the department, campus, or community or leadership in professional associations.

A systemic approach to promoting service-learning at a teaching institution links the three components of teaching, research, and service. It can be woven into a campus's culture in such a way that it is consistent with university goals, such as student retention. It serves faculty and students most effectively when it is connected to multiyear priorities that seek to improve institutional effectiveness, such as the assessment of student learning.

This chapter is directed toward faculty who function as advocates or champions of service-learning at a teaching institution. They are presumed to be familiar with service-learning, having incorporated it into at least one course. They are now promoting service-learning to colleagues as an extension of their values regarding teaching and learning. These faculty members have probably embraced other forms of experiential learning as strategies

NEW DIRECTIONS FOR HIGHER EDUCATION, no. 114, Summer 2001 © John Wiley & Sons, Inc.

to engage students at both cognitive and affective levels. They believe in the importance of reflection and self-assessment as a vehicle for transforming student perspectives, and they believe in the power of teaching institutions to produce an engaged citizenry. They promote a service ethic as a natural part of being an educated person. Service-learning is conceptualized not only as a pedagogy but also as a movement with the potential to contribute to a healthier society by intentionally confronting students with issues of diversity, social justice, and the ethical use of discipline-based knowledge.

Challenges and Solutions

Faculty who are promoting service-learning at their teaching institutions face a number of challenges. Each represents a potential barrier since it represents resistance to the initial use of service-learning in a course, a department, or a program. Here I offer potential solutions for faculty members who are working to educate their colleagues and administrators to gain support for their use of service-learning or who want to access campus resources and support for service-learning.

Challenge One: "We already do that." Faculty members invited to incorporate service-learning into existing courses often respond, "We already do that." They dismiss the idea because they see internships, practica, and fieldwork courses as service-learning. Courses bearing those titles are separate from core curriculum and are ideologically bracketed into a separate category of teaching and learning experiences by being assigned to faculty or staff. Someone else is seen as the resident expert in working with the community.

In fact, there is a continuum of community-based learning opportunities, and service-learning is distinct from internships, practica, and fieldwork. For example, an internship is usually a capstone or final experience that offers students a chance to use what they have learned throughout a major to connect with career opportunities or begin their professional networking. There is often little connection with a classroom experience or seminar in which those experiences can be connected to course readings.

By contrast, service-learning can be used in any credit-bearing course to engage students in a community-based service experience connected to the learning outcomes of the course. Students participate in reflection exercises designed to enhance the learning outcomes of the course. The hours of service are assigned as relevant experience, just as chapters of a textbook would be assigned as reading. The completion of the minimum number of hours serves as the basis for an examination of the course content, as it was applied or revealed through the service experience.

Solution to Challenge One. Definitions of service-learning must be clear. Faculty and administrators must conceptualize service-learning as being situated at the midpoint of an experiential learning continuum, anchored by pure service or volunteerism on one end and by pure practice or internships on the other. The inclusion of service as a vehicle for improved learning must be separate and distinct from preprofessional or capstone training experiences. It must also be distinct from community service or volunteerism. Hours of service constitute one of many assigned activities in the course and do not represent the entire focus for the course.

This challenge is a basic one that can be addressed through faculty governance units, including the academic senate or related committees that create policy for academic standards.

Challenge Two: "Service is volunteerism. We're lowering our standards to give academic credit for service." This reaction to the use of service for learning can be related to the issue of definition, but it is broader. People who articulate this point of view are among the strongest advocates of academic standards and those who truly care about protecting the reputation of the institution and its ability to attract high-quality students and faculty. They do not want to see the curriculum watered down and do not want the institution to be viewed as one that passes out easy credit for spending a few hours volunteering.

Faculty and administrators who argue that service-learning lowers standards are also often implying that knowledge is generated solely through contact with professors. Representatives of some disciplines will argue that classroom time is essential to creating successful graduates and majors. They see service as taking students' time and attention away from learning course content.

Solution to Challenge Two. Professors can address this challenge by working with those charged with policies for academic standards to produce a policy on the academic standards for the use of service-learning. The policy can link the learning outcomes for the course with participation in service, so that the course content is applied. The policy developed on our campus offers an opportunity to communicate the conditions under which a faculty member is justified in using the term *service-learning* in the syllabus for a course.

Another solution to this challenge is to reference research by cognitive and educational psychologists suggesting that the application of academic content in real-world problem-solving situations results in learning that is retained longer and can be more easily transferred to new situations. In addition, research on service-learning suggests that it improves critical-thinking skills, a valued outcome for graduates of most teaching institutions, regardless of major.

Challenge Three: "Service-learning takes too much time and effort. We can't add it to the faculty workload!" This challenge, like the others, is a reflection of the campus culture in teaching institutions—a culture that often advances new institutional improvements by increasing faculty workloads. Administrators are often reluctant to create conflict by asking faculty to accept assignments above and beyond their standard teaching loads.

Teaching institutions often disagree about whether curricular innovations should be top down or bottom up in their flow. Faculty may resent a mandate to incorporate something new into the classroom; an innovation advanced by an individual must be marketed and embraced by peers. Although the institution values innovation, the acceptance of new practices for teaching and learning must be consistent with longstanding practices rather than represent something so completely different that it is an add-on to faculty workloads.

Solution to Challenge Three. One solution to this challenge is to conceptualize service-learning as a tool to achieve other academic goals. For example, what if a faculty member started using service-learning in a course and his or her teaching evaluations improved, which in turn helped that person in the retention and promotion process? And what if the faculty member then presented this outcome at a discipline-based conference or wrote up the method and results in one of the major journals in her or his field?

How to get support at the level of department heads and deans is more complex. Service-learning can have an impact on retention rates or time to graduation. It can be included in outreach and marketing pieces designed to attract more students to the program, department, or school. Service-learning can improve the overall image of the institution as civic minded, caring, connected, and engaged with the communities adjacent to campus.

Faculty members can also look around to identify the hot issues on campus. Often multiyear initiatives become priorities, attracting planning and resources. And often these initiatives are market driven or emerge as responses to external stakeholders, such as legislators concerned with accountability or broader movements in national higher education. Examples include the increased use of technology or the study of some aspect of institutional effectiveness through ongoing research and longitudinal study of the campus population. It is critical that service-learners partner with those engaged with other campus priorities and make those vital connections to advance the goals of the university.

There are many examples. For instance, if the campus has a faculty development center, an examination of current programming can reveal priorities to faculty, since those offerings are likely to be well attended. This organizational unit can help offer training, brown-bag lunches, informal workshops, or faculty mentoring around service-learning issues. Service-learning is then helping faculty improve and advance their careers, while contributing to the overall satisfaction with the institution.

Consider some ways in which this might happen. Faculty in the visual arts may work with community partners to have students produce new World Wide Web sites for nonprofit organizations. A biology professor might have students teach science units in a middle school. A computer science professor might have students in local senior centers help older adults access health-related information on their own medical conditions or prescribed medications. Child development students might help elementary school students in after-school programs with age-appropriate activities.

These activities will likely produce visible evidence of the university's commitment to being engaged with the community through authentic partnerships. They generate energy and excitement about the process of learning for students who are motivated through active learning strategies. Commitment to the department and institution often increases, and student course evaluations mirror that commitment. Service-learning thus can increase retention, as well as the numbers of majors or applicants. The assessment of service-learning can be incorporated into a broader assessment plan for departments or colleges.

First-year programming is also a good match for service-learning, particularly when incorporated into learning communities. Linked courses in learning communities can include a service-learning experience, which is used as text in both courses, such as political science and a writing course. Students see this applied, experiential learning as powerful and meaningful. Classroom discussions become more personally relevant, and students build a sense of community with one another through shared work in local nonprofit organizations.

Challenge Four: "Service-learning will not help with retention, promotion, and tenure." Junior faculty members need to focus on activities that will advance their careers. In most cases, personnel guidelines and policies do not include provisions for the use of applied scholarship or alternative forms of community-based projects. Research that takes place in the community is often viewed as service, not scholarship. These are valid and realistic concerns raised by faculty members who feel vulnerable if they consider innovation in their teaching strategies. Senior faculty often communicate a sense of disapproval for anything other than traditional research agendas.

Solution to Challenge Four. Teaching institutions can take the lead in producing peer-reviewed service-learning articles that showcase innovation in teaching and evidence of improved learning. Faculty members need help in learning how to publish what they do in a research-based format that applies a methodology for data collection and analysis. By learning to apply a scholarship of engaged teaching and pedagogy, faculty can link these two agendas to make a deliberate connection between classroom practices and the advancement of knowledge in their fields. Across disciplines, faculty can study student-learning outcomes related to the use of service-learning or pose research questions related to the academic content of the course that become publications for a larger audience of their colleagues.

Faculty members also can conceptualize classrooms as learning laboratories. A teaching institution can help facilitate the development of a faculty culture in which self-reflection and self-assessment of teaching and learning are linked to accreditation systems and other university programs for the study of institutional effectiveness. Faculty can study which of the variables included in their service-learning course produced the best outcomes and study the effects of various interventions over time. Do class size, the number of community partners, working alone or in teams, or the number of hours of service provided make a difference in grade-point averages or measures of student learning?

Recognition events that identify those who engaged in service and service-learning also assist faculty in their professional growth and development. Acknowledgment of faculty in campus publications or public relations pieces that describe innovative work with community partners builds the positive reputations of faculty who foster caring relationships with the community.

Challenge Five: "We're not here to teach morality or social justice!" This challenge comes from those who feel pressured to use limited class time to make sure students are learning the knowledge base of their discipline. These faculty members are not interested in encouraging students to engage in discussions of moral or ethical issues. They do not see such discussions as part of their role. Furthermore, not all faculty members are equally comfortable discussing such issues. The personal or provocative nature of these discussions may create classroom management problems or impede the faculty member's ability to reach other specified or predetermined learning goals.

Solution to Challenge Five. It is highly unlikely that all professors will someday incorporate the use of service-learning in all their courses. Some departments will choose to use service-learning only in upper-division courses.

A number of disciplines have professional associations with codes of ethics that articulate the proper use of discipline-based practices. There is a growing trend across disciplines to frame requirements for membership in associations around codes of acceptable and responsible behavior, including the socially or environmentally responsible use of a knowledge base. Whether they are psychologists, accountants, or biologists, contemporary professionals are confronted with the need to take proper care in the application of their craft. Faculty care that their graduates not just finish the degree but be able to perform at a high level of competence that reflects on the institution and their own educational program. Service-learning can contribute to the success and reputation of a company, a corporation, and a community.

Institutional Partnerships at a Teaching Institution

Faculty who advocate the increased use of service-learning by their colleagues need to develop creative partnerships with institutional programs or organizational units. Who can contribute to the success of service-learning as a permanent fixture in a teaching institution? What units have goals that can be met through the use of service-learning?

Faculty governance bodies are key to setting policy for all things that relate to teaching, and the leaders of those groups are highly influential in gaining acceptance for service-learning. They must understand that academic credit is earned through learning, not service. Students do not get their proverbial ticket punched by spending a predetermined number of hours in a nonprofit service organization. They must engage in critical, complex discoveries that reveal themselves in classroom discussions or written assignments.

Among the work-study offices that have designated funding for service-related initiatives are America Reads and Counts, AmeriCorps, and VISTA. Students can engage in service-learning while satisfying work-study requirements. Faculty members can hire work-study students to supervise or train service-learning students. Work-study students can help with the work of organizing paperwork and tracking systems for service hours or making connections and introductions with community-based site supervisors.

Student affairs professionals are often responsible for student-run community service programs or outreach efforts in the community. They can help faculty begin using service-learning by providing contacts with those who have a previous service relationship with the university. They are also interested in the personal development of students and often have links to leadership training or career development activities that can be linked to service-learning courses.

Faculty advocates can promote service-learning in other ways. They can find out if there is a tradition of volunteerism or community service among students, staff, and faculty on the campus. Attitudes toward service or participation in community-based activities can be collected and used as data to study student interest or openness to service-learning as part of their expectations for a satisfying college experience.

A faculty development center or center for teaching and learning can help to rally faculty and administrative support for service-learning. Initial support might come in the form of advertising workshops or securing space for service-learning training. Later, those charged with orientation for new faculty might make time available in their programming so all new faculty hear about ways to get involved with service-learning.

The career planning and placement center is also useful. Service-learning is valuable in challenging students to consider alternative majors and careers and is often identified as a tool for enhancing career development. Faculty can find support in identifying community partners through contacts the career center staff have already made with nonprofit organizations as potential employers.

A university's internship center often has persons with expertise in student preparation or issues of risk management. They can train faculty who are new to service-learning or help form partnerships across campus for service-learning as a respectable alternative to experiential education in an internship.

Faculty members interested in promoting service-learning can also find out what kind of pathways and associations exist with the university's alumni. Existing chapters of alumni organized around a major or school might provide useful contacts for setting up service-learning experiences. Alumni are often eager to mentor and connect with students and want to have an organized, structured way to do that; service-learning provides such a framework that includes faculty support. Alumni can become champions of service-learning and enlist the support not only of other alumni but also of the university foundation or advancement offices.

Faculty members need to find out what their campus outreach programs are and ask if they can include information on service-learning opportunities in off-campus presentations to prospective students who may be looking for a university that promotes personal development, career exploration, and academic success.

Faculty advocates can also encourage their colleagues to visit Web sites that provide information on service-learning. Key examples include the resources available through the American Association for Higher Education (AAHE), Campus Compact, the National Clearinghouse for Service Learning, the Invisible College, National Association for Experiential Education (NSEE), or the resources available through the Chancellor's Office of the California State University (CSU) system. AAHE has discipline-based monographs and a consultation team. Campus Compact has a tool kit with resources for training and development, and the CSU listserv offers information on infrastructure, teaching issues, and more. Faculty can then showcase these resources for their colleagues to promote the use of service-learning without having to build it from the ground up or having to develop all the tools in isolation.

Finally, service-learning can be launched and promoted through grants at the state or national level, as well as through foundation support for pilot projects. Help is available in locating appropriate funding sources, collaborating on proposal writing, or even partnering with other faculty to promote service-learning within a campuswide program. Some institutions have a faculty research office or staff who work with grants and contracts and can provide assistance.

Faculty members can study their institution to see how service-learning can contribute to exciting projects, key agendas, or university priorities. Service-learning cannot be effective as a stand-alone program or remain separate from the day-to-day life of the institution. It must be embedded into the university to foster a service ethic as part of the identity of an educated person.

Conclusion

Faculty members in teaching institutions can promote the use of service-learning by anticipating challenges and preparing solutions to address them. These solutions must acknowledge the institution's goals as well as the multiple demands placed on faculty to teach, publish, and engage in service.

The definition for service-learning on campus must be clear. How is service-learning the same as or different from other forms of experiential education or community-based learning such as fieldwork, practica, or internships? What policies define the use of those terms? Once those definitions are in place, they will guide the formation of related issues such as academic standards and an appropriate infrastructure for campuswide visibility. The development of resources for this infrastructure must blend with other university goals, planning, and resource development plans and the identity of the specific teaching institution. Partnering with various organizational units on campus that will share in reaping the rewards of a satisfying service-learning experience creates long-term investment in service-learning as part of the university's identity. Relationships with alumni and community partners enhance the reputation of the university as responsive to community needs and willing to invest the intellectual resources of faculty and students alike in addressing real-world problems.

Structures for service-learning then lead to processes such as student preparation and orientation, risk management and liability procedures, criteria for approved sites, and a tracking system or database.

Finally, faculty members in teaching institutions can incorporate service-learning into their research agendas. Various levels of scholarship are available, including the assessment of student learning in a single course and the investigation of the impact of service-learning on faculty, students, and community partners or on measures of community well-being. The unit of analysis can be set at the level of a single section of a course or longitudinal changes in indicators of health or well-being collected by policymakers or legislatures. Service-learning also lends itself well to interdisciplinary research, when students from various disciplines are teamed at a single site working on a single, complex problem related to the human condition. Service-learning scholarship that contributes to the knowledge base of a discipline can also encourage a lifelong habit of civic engagement for students in teaching institutions.

KATHY O'BYRNE is associate professor of counseling and director of programs for freshmen at California State University, Fullerton.

10

Institutionalizing service-learning at a liberal arts college may not raise unique issues, but the size and focus of such an institution do add defining considerations.

Humanistic Learning and Service-Learning at the Liberal Arts College

Edward Zlotkowski

Although service-learning as an academic movement is little more than a decade old, its connection with humanistic learning is complex. While it is often said to have its natural base in the humanities and the social sciences, this is only partially true. Core humanistic disciplines like philosophy, history, and literary studies have contributed relatively little to the movement's growth and increasing sophistication. Indeed, literary studies may be the least well represented of all the more common academic disciplines. Also poorly represented are math and most natural sciences, with the important exception of environmental studies and environmental biology. According to Campus Compact, the five fields where service-learning is most likely to occur are education, sociology, psychology, counseling and social work, and business and accounting (Rothman, 1998). On the other hand, the largest category of Compact membership is the traditional liberal arts institution (Rothman, 1998). This is not surprising. Another higher education association, the Council of Independent Colleges, whose membership is made up exclusively of private liberal arts colleges, has noted, in conjunction with its most recent service-learning grant competition, that

> private liberal arts institutions . . . not only consider student learning their preeminent goal but indeed set their sights for this learning intentionally high, nurturing students to aspire not just for jobs but for meaningful careers that can contribute to society, not just for a knowledge of civics but for sustained involvement in responsible and active citizenship. The intent is that graduates should find a moral imperative in improving their world. [Garth, 1999, p. 9]

In other words, the very mission of the liberal arts college is in many ways deeply congruous with the goals of service-learning, which include, in any given instance, "further understanding of the course content, a broader appreciation of the discipline, and an enhanced sense of civic responsibility" (Bringle and Hatcher, 1996, p. 222).

What is one to make of this discrepancy: that the arts and sciences at the very core of the liberal arts college—the humanities and the natural sciences—are precisely those areas of the curriculum that have shown the least interest in an educational approach so remarkably congruent with the core missions of their own institutions? That the philosophy department or the chemistry department at a research university should show little interest in "a broader appreciation of the discipline" and "an enhanced sense of civic responsibility" is unfortunate but not anomalous, given their institution's professed priorities, but in the case of liberal arts colleges, precisely the opposite is the case.

However one explains this puzzle, it is clear that addressing it is fundamental to the creation of a successful service-learning program at a liberal arts college. Just as a business school cannot build a successful long-term service-learning program on the strength of its nonbusiness courses or a school of engineering around its nonengineering curriculum, so a liberal arts college that relies primarily on its social science, business, and preprofessional programs will not succeed in developing a service-learning dimension that has the legitimacy—and hence the resources—to contribute in a substantive, integrated way to the institution's commitment to liberal learning (Zlotkowski, 1998). Indeed, it will forfeit the opportunity to develop an approach to liberal learning particularly appropriate for today's students and today's society.

Perhaps no one else has made a more compelling case for such a claim than Lee Shulman, professor of education at Stanford University and president of the Carnegie Foundation for the Advancement of Teaching and Learning. In an article entitled "Professing the Liberal Arts" (1997), Shulman asks what liberal learning might look like if it were treated as a profession. Shulman's understanding of what it means to "profess"—and not merely to study—the liberal arts would seem to accord particularly well with a society that desperately needs to bring its intellectual resources to bear on both public and proprietary concerns, as well as with a student generation that demonstrates a marked preference for "sensory learning patterns"—that is, learning that privileges "the concrete, the practical, and the immediate" (Schroeder, 1993).

Such an updated understanding of the liberal arts may diverge widely from more genteel notions of knowledge for its own sake, but such notions themselves diverge from the moral and civic goals that characterize the mission statements of most American liberal arts colleges. Indeed, as Holland (1999) has pointed out, a "review of mission fosters a rediscovery of [an] institution's historical origins that typically involved a more interactive relationship with the people and issues of its region or community" (p. 49). For evidence of the connection between the liberal arts and service, we need only scan the mission statements posted on the Web by liberal arts colleges such as Oberlin and Bates, as well as research on the history of liberal arts colleges (for example, Church and Sedlak, 1989; Potts, 1989).

What Is to Be Done?

We must ask specifically what steps a liberal arts college should take if it wishes to develop an academically and socially effective service-learning program.

Task One: Revisit the College's Mission. The first task is revisit the college's mission, recognizing not only the vision it allegedly serves but also the extent to which all its current programs, particularly its curricular programs, contribute concretely and specifically to the realization of that vision. Such a task is far more difficult than it may at first seem, for it requires great honesty and, hence, great effort and determination. The kind of trickle-down contributions to which we have all become so accustomed will do little to help the clarification process.

Recognizing how the activities of individual departments and individual faculty members do or do not contribute in a verifiable way to service-related goals articulated in a college's mission statement is the necessary first step to creating genuine congruence between the two. For this reason, some of the most successful service-learning programs have begun with a rigorous, comprehensive audit of the ways in which individuals and units already contribute to and partner with the off-campus community. The power of such audits is that they uncover not only deficiencies to be corrected but also opportunities to build on. In other words, they make possible effective strategic planning.

Task Two: Assemble Resources. The second task follows directly from the first: having revisited the college's mission and carefully inventoried the specific contributions faculty and academic units currently make to the actualization of that mission, the institution must assemble whatever resources are needed to deal with the opportunities and gaps identified. Such resources generally fall into two different but complementary categories. The first is an effective system for supporting faculty partnering efforts. A second set of resources is also needed, and these may or may not be the responsibility of the centralized support system. Faculty need help not only with the noncurricular dimensions of partnering but also with access to the work of colleagues in the same field at other comparable institutions. If, for example, the natural sciences have been slow to develop partnering and outreach initiatives, the problem may well be that individuals in that area have no idea what such initiatives would look like and how they might contribute to student learning. Professors can begin finding such assistance in the American Association for Higher Education's

(AAHE) eighteen-volume series on service-learning in the disciplines (1997–2000), as well as numerous resources developed by Campus Compact and national disciplinary associations.

Task Three: Connect Service-Learning to Similar Concerns. A third task can in some ways be considered a subset of the second. Efforts to introduce faculty to service-learning should seek to make connections between service-learning and other progressive pedagogical strategies and contemporary concerns. To the extent that service-learning is seen as another add-on, it will have difficulty developing deep faculty support. However, if it can be linked to other institutional and disciplinary priorities and presented as a way to consolidate rather than inflate the faculty workload, its appeal will be immediately enhanced. To make such a case, one needs only to turn again to the AAHE series on service-learning in the disciplines, for the eighteen volumes are full of examples of how service-learning can provide a vehicle for collaborative learning, problem-based learning, multiculturalism, learning communities, critical thinking, and enhanced communication skills. For example, Simmons (2000) has argued that service-learning raises student motivation, and Ward (1999) shows that service-learning can promote a coherent curriculum.

Task Four: Form a Plan for Faculty Development. Accomplishing the second and third tasks implies a significant investment in faculty development, and thus we can identify the formulation and implementation of a comprehensive faculty development plan as the fourth task. Most liberal arts colleges that have created service-learning programs have at some time offered small grants to faculty willing to design new service-learning courses or course components. Far fewer institutions have given sufficient thought to how to leverage the results of such efforts for maximum advantage. For example, designing a service-learning course and teaching it only once is not calculated to provide a reliable basis for assessing what that newly designed course can contribute to either student learning or curricular goals. Since very few faculty members have been trained in the theory and practice of experiential education, chances are the first time they offer a service-learning course, their experience will be highly experimental. What is needed—indeed, required—is a stipulation that grant recipients correct and refine their initial efforts in subsequent semesters.

In a similar vein, faculty development efforts are rarely thought of as involving more than individual faculty members. Only recently have there been forms of support that target the participation of entire departments. This does not mean that every member of a department is expected to use service-learning, only that the unit of responsibility developing service-learning opportunities is the department as a single curricular unit. Where among a department's offerings does service-learning make the most sense? How can it complement more traditional pedagogies? How can it be developed and offered in such a way that it does not remain dependent on a single individual's teaching schedule? How can the department recognize—and even institutionalize—the work involved in maintaining quality community partnerships?

For a departmentally focused development strategy to succeed, it may well be necessary for the college to reach out to departments in new ways. DeZure (1996), commenting on faculty development in general, has noted the importance of discipline-specific development. Hence we return to the second task: assembling the resources needed to make conversations about service-learning clear and cogent on a disciplinary level. This, in turn, means discipline-related concepts and models.

It is at this point that the liberal arts college as a distinctive educational context assumes special importance. Although all of the suggestions offered in this chapter can be considered generic in that they identify strategies that can be modified to fit most kinds of higher education institutions, both the mandate to use those strategies and the circumstances that define their use are especially encouraging at liberal arts colleges. I have already referenced the fact that the mission statements of most liberal arts colleges are articulated in language remarkably resonant with the aims of service-learning. The same can be said for the institutional circumstances that define learning at these institutions: a focus on teaching as the single most important faculty responsibility, small class size and extensive faculty-student interaction, active student engagement in the learning process, an emphasis on community, student and faculty populations sufficiently small to make coherent programming, active experimentation, and meaningful collaboration.

Implementation of a departmentally focused faculty development effort can be viewed as a strategy of special, if not exclusive, significance in this context. Freed from the constraints of conflicting institutional priorities and unwieldy size, the liberal arts department can identify precisely the most effective way in which it can use service-learning to fulfill its mission and nurture its students' growth. However, just as the moral and civic dimensions of a school's mission statement demand more than rhetorical articulation, so the implementation of an effective service-learning program requires more than a targeted faculty development agenda. It also demands a willingness to recognize, within the context of a school's promotion and tenure system, the contributions of those most responsible for making service-learning part of an institution's curricular effort.

Task Five: Reward Faculty Who Use Service-Learning. This task targets the development of procedures to recognize and reward such contributions, to make explicit the institution's commitment to supporting excellence in community-based work. Although liberal arts colleges already have a long tradition of recognizing teaching excellence in their promotion and tenure guidelines, those guidelines may provide no easy way to capture the special quality and value of community-based teaching activities and by default may wind up relegating all community-based work to an inappropriate service category. The extent of this problem has only recently begun to be recognized and addressed as academic institutions of all kinds revisit their guidelines to make clear the kinds of community-based work that can and should be valued as contributing to the scholarship of teaching. At a minimum, it is important that an institution's evaluation documents carefully distinguish between service-learning as an academic undertaking and traditional forms of community service. Both the New England Resource Center for Higher Education and Campus Compact have posted examples of revised promotion and tenure guidelines on their Web sites.

But all responsibility in this area does not rest with the institution. Faculty practitioners need to learn to evaluate and document their work in a way that can be appreciated by faculty peers used to more traditional, exclusively classroom-based pedagogies. Fortunately, important new resources to help faculty do just that have begun appearing on a regular basis. In addition to the AAHE series is a collection of model syllabi posted on the Campus Compact Web site, as well as Driscoll and Lynton's *Making Outreach Visible: A Guide to Documenting Professional Service and Outreach* (1999). Individual state compacts such as Indiana (Center for Public Service and Leadership, 1999) and Ohio (Falbo, n.d.) have also made available faculty guidebooks that directly address issues such as documentation and evaluation. Indeed, the once frequently heard complaint that we do not know how to assess the academic value of service-learning has ceased to be valid. Individual faculty members, committees, and institutions may not know, but the knowledge is available.

The New American College

James Carignan (1998), dean of the college at Bates College, has argued that "learning is rooted in place" and that service-learning "connects teachers and students to place and contributes mightily to positive community relations essential to this dimension of learning" (p. 41). Carignan's observation about learning, service-learning, and place would seem to lead in two directions. First, it suggests a renewed appreciation of the specific and the concrete as fundamental to liberal learning. In an age increasingly dominated by both globalization and technology, it is easy to forget the importance of the local. But if recognition of the particular, the concrete, and the individual as central to both civic and moral traditions is to survive anywhere, surely it must be in liberal arts colleges. Here, after all, we find most clearly maintained the tradition of liberal learning that the earliest colleges in the United States inherited from England. Indeed, as values of instant access, instant information, and digital standardization become increasingly widespread, it is imperative that sustained and deliberate attention be paid to those forms of knowing that do not conform to the dominant technological paradigm.

"But why should this imply service-learning?" some will ask. "Is not respect for the idiosyncratic and the particular embedded in the humanities ipso facto?" Perhaps. But even if the future of humanistic study is not at stake in whether service-learning is embraced, the ability of the humanities to take root in new learners and to exercise a palpable influence on the way they live their lives may be at stake. As Ewell (1997) and others report, application and experience are not incidental to in-depth understanding. When what students learn in their courses can be deliberately reflected, refracted, and refined in nonacademic experiences, many discover for the first time what being liberally educated is all about.

A second direction in which Carignan's observation leads is the service dimension of service-learning. I have already noted how common it is for the mission statement of liberal arts institutions to stress "moral and civic leadership," "contributions to society," and "education linked to service." There is, however, no reason that such desirables need be seen as belonging primarily to the future. Many liberal arts colleges began and grew in close connection with their surrounding communities (Church and Sedlack, 1989) and to this day continue to play an important economic and cultural role in those communities. Why should that role not also include a well-developed social dimension, whereby faculty and students work together with community members to harness their collective expertise to local issues and public problem solving? It was precisely such an academy-community collaboration that Boyer (1994) had in mind when he sketched his vision of "the New American College" as "an institution that supports teaching and selectively supports research, while also taking special pride in its ability to connect thought to action, theory to practice" (p. A48). In Boyer's vision, students would learn in the community, and practitioners in the community would bring their knowledge to the campus. Clearly, such a vision can provide a moral, social, and intellectual foundation for the kind of "good town-gown relationships" Carignan has in mind—relationships that suggest neither noblesse oblige nor opportunistic public relations. It is, in fact, a compelling articulation of what is possible when the potential of service-learning is linked with the mission, orientation, and resources of the liberal arts college.

References

Boyer, E. "Creating the New American College." *Chronicle of Higher Education*, Mar. 9, 1994, p. A48.

Bringle, R. G., and Hatcher, J. A. "Implementing Service Learning in Higher Education." *Journal of Higher Education*, 1996, 67, 221–239.

Carignan, J. "Curriculum and Community Connection: The Center for Service-Learning at Bates College." In E. Zlotkowski (ed.), *Successful Service-Learning Programs: New Models of Excellence in Higher Education*. Bolton, Mass.: Anker, 1998.

Center for Public Service and Leadership. *Service at Indiana University: Defining, Documenting, and Evaluating*. Indianapolis, Ind.: Center for Public Service and Leadership, 1999.

Church, R. L., and Sedlak, M. W. "The Antebellum College and Academy." In L. F. Goodchild and H. S. Wechsler (eds.), *The ASHE Reader on the History of Higher Education*. New York: Ginn Press, 1989.

DeZure, D. "Closer to the Disciplines: A Model for Improving Teaching Within Departments." *AAHE Bulletin*, 1996, 8(6), 9–12.

Driscoll, A., and Lynton, E. A. *Making Outreach Visible.* Washington, D.C.: American Association for Higher Education, 1999.

Ewell, P. "Organizing for Learning." *AAHE Bulletin,* 1997, *9,* 3–6.

Falbo, M.C. *Serving to Learn: A Faculty Guide to Service Learning.* Granville, Ohio: Ohio Campus Compact, n.d.

Garth, R. *Engaging Communities and Campuses.* Washington, D.C.: Council of Independent Colleges, 1999.

Holland, B. A. "From Murky to Meaningful: The Role of Mission in Institutional Change." In R. G. Bringle, R. Games, and E. A. Malloy (eds.), *Colleges and Universities as Citizens.* Needham Heights, Mass.: Allyn and Bacon, 1999.

Potts, D. B. "'College Enthusiasm!' as Public Response: 1800–1860." In L. F. Goodchild and H. S. Wechsler (eds.), *The ASHE Reader on the History of Higher Education.* New York: Ginn Press, 1989.

Rothman, M. (ed.). *Service Matters.* Providence, R.I.: Campus Compact, 1998.

Schroeder, C. C. "New Students—New Learning Styles." *Change,* Sept.–Oct. 1993, pp. 21–26.

Shulman, L. S. "Professing the Liberal Arts." In R. Orrill (ed.), *Education and Democracy: Re-imagining Liberal Learning in America.* New York: College Entrance Examination Board, 1997.

Simmons, J. A. "An Environmental Science Approach to Service-Learning in Biology." In D. C. Brubaker and J. H. Ostroff (eds.), *Life, Learning, and Community: Concepts and Models for Service-Learning in Biology.* Washington, D.C.: American Association for Higher Education, 2000.

Ward, H. "Why Is Service-Learning So Pervasive in Environmental Studies Programs?" In H. Ward (ed.), *Acting Locally: Concepts and Models for Service-Learning in Environmental Studies.* Washington, D.C.: American Association for Higher Education, 1999.

Zlotkowski, E. "Introduction: A New Model of Excellence." In E. Zlotkowski (ed.), *Successful Service-Learning Programs: New Models of Excellence in Higher Education.* Bolton, Mass.: Anker, 1998.

EDWARD ZLOTKOWSKI, senior faculty fellow at Campus Compact and professor of English at Bentley College, has served as general editor of the American Association for Higher Education's eighteen-volume series on service-learning in the academic disciplines.

11

Resources for effective teaching in service-learning courses are essential for professors new to service-learning.

Additional Resources

Elaine K. Ikeda

"Service-learning: What is it? Why should I consider integrating service-learning into my course, and how might it fit?" These are questions that faculty new to service-learning might ask. Where can they find the answers to these questions? This chapter offers some resources for faculty initiates to service-learning that may assist them in understanding service-learning and the role it can have in enhancing learning among college students.

In recent years, there has been an explosion of information about service-learning and effective pedagogy. The availability of service-learning models at different types of institutions has grown. Entire conferences devoted to it are now commonplace, and a burgeoning array of literature focuses on service-learning. Yet among the ever-expanding bookshelves and file cabinets, a cadre of works remains at the core. These works, which are commonly recommended by veterans to new faculty interested in service-learning, are highlighted in this chapter.

An excellent resource for faculty new to service-learning is Campus Compact's *Introduction to Service-Learning Toolkit* (1999), with valuable readings and useful resources designed specifically for faculty. With a compilation of writings by recognized leaders in the service-learning and experiential education field, this book provides a well-rounded overview of many of the essential issues related to teaching and learning in higher education and service-learning. Sections address definitions and principles, theory, pedagogy, community partnerships, reflection, academic culture, student development, assessment, model programs, curriculum, and promotion and tenure.

Each section begins with a series of questions that challenge readers to reflect and relate the readings to their own teaching experience, academic discipline, campus, and community. A recommended reading list at the end of each section provides additional resources.

NEW DIRECTIONS FOR HIGHER EDUCATION, no. 114, Summer 2001 © John Wiley & Sons, Inc.   97

Another book with a broad overview of service-learning that is useful to faculty new to the field is *Service-Learning in Higher Education: Concepts and Practices* (1996), by Jacoby and others. This book demonstrates how service-learning relates to teaching, learning, and research in higher education. Of particular interest to faculty are Chapters Seven and Twelve.

In Chapter Seven, "Service-Learning in the Curriculum," Sandra Eons and Marie Troppe describe several methods of integrating service-learning into the curriculum, including fourth-credit option and stand-alone service-learning modules, introductory service-learning courses, courses linking service and leadership, service as a required or optional course component, and service as a course requirement. The chapter also discusses service-learning as a graduation requirement, disciplinary capstone courses, and service-learning majors and minors. Specific institutional examples are provided for each of the identified models.

Chapter Twelve, "Issues Related to Integrating Service-Learning into the Curriculum," addresses some important issues for faculty to consider in seeking to integrate service-learning into their teaching. The author of this chapter, Keith Morton, raises philosophical and practical questions, such as, What is service? Will the service be required or optional? How much service should be asked of students? In addition, he discusses issues relating to institutional support for curricular service-learning, including faculty development, faculty assistance, and policies supporting service-learning.

In 1999, Eyler and Giles published *Where's the Learning in Service Learning?* and thereby made a great contribution to the relevant literature. This book is packed with research evidence about the effectiveness of service-learning and also filled with practical information. As Alexander Astin states in the foreword for the book, "A particular strength of this book is that it focuses on both the outcomes and the process of service learning" (p. xii). Of particular interest for college faculty are Chapters Eight and Nine. Chapter Eight focuses on providing information about program characteristics (such as placement quality, reflection, and community voice) that help form positive and successful service-learning experiences for students and faculty. Chapter Nine provides a more in-depth look at strengthening the role of service in the curriculum and operationalizes many of the program characteristics cited in the previous chapter. The book concludes with a detailed description of the two research projects that produced the data for this book. This information is helpful for faculty wishing to engage in service-learning research.

Another excellent resource for faculty new to service-learning is *Praxis I: A Faculty Casebook on Community Service Learning* (1993), edited by Howard. All of the chapters are written by University of Michigan faculty who have taught community service-learning courses. This book, the first in a three-part series, was one of the first to provide valuable pedagogical models for faculty. Although the models presented in the book are discipline based, the pedagogical issues raised can be applied to other service-learning courses.

Praxis I is divided into three main sections. The first section provides an overview of community service-learning, reviewing general principles and information regarding the design and implementation of service-learning courses across the disciplines. The second section contains eleven models of undergraduate service-learning courses. The last section contains graduate models of service-learning courses.

Howard edits another valuable resource, the *Michigan Journal of Community Service-Learning*. First published in 1994 and produced annually since then, this journal is well respected in the field of service-learning. Each issue contains articles on research, pedagogy, and other issues related to service-learning.

Another powerful resource for faculty is *A Practitioner's Guide to Reflection in Service-Learning: Student Voices and Reflections* (1996), by Eyler, Giles, and Schmiede. The authors collected in-depth qualitative data, which led to the development of this practical guide. This guidebook has been used to train faculty, community partners, and community service-learning staff in how to engage students in critical reflection about their service-learning experience. It is filled with exercises, experiences, sample assignments, and case study interview instruments. The guidebook provides step-by-step suggestions for sequencing reflection, as well as various modes for facilitating reflection (writing, reading, telling, and doing). Each chapter contains a helpful list of references and resources.

In an effort to provide focused resources for faculty engaged in or considering service-learning, the American Association for Higher Education (AAHE) has published an eighteen-monograph series on service-learning in various disciplines: accounting, biology, communications, composition, engineering, environmental studies, history, management, medical education, nursing, peace studies, philosophy, political science, psychology, sociology, Spanish, teacher education, and women's studies. Edited by Edward Zlotkowski, each discipline-specific volume consists of ten to twenty scholarly essays, both theoretical and pedagogical, offering rich and provocative discussions on integrating service-learning in the discipline. The monographs also contain program descriptions, course materials, and annotated bibliographies. The series is not intended to serve as an introduction to generic service-learning but rather focuses on the integration of service-learning within specific disciplines.

This chapter does not review the plethora of high-quality service-learning articles available in journals and books on related topics such as civic engagement, social capital, the teaching and learning paradigm, and faculty development. In addition, faculty should seek out resources from their disciplinary associations or from organizations that specialize in serving specific types of higher education institutions, such as American Association of Community Colleges.

References

Campus Compact. *Introduction to Service-Learning Toolkit.* Providence, R.I.: Brown University, 1999.

Eyler, J., and Giles, D. E., Jr. *Where's the Learning in Service-Learning?* San Francisco: Jossey-Bass, 1999.

Eyler, J., Giles, D. E., Jr., and Schmiede, A. *A Practitioner's Guide to Reflection in Service-Learning: Student Voices and Reflections.* Nashville, Tenn.: Vanderbilt University, 1996.

Howard, J.P.F. *Praxis I: A Faculty Casebook on Community Service Learning.* Ann Arbor, Mich.: OCSL Press, 1993.

Jacoby, B., and Associates. *Service-Learning in Higher Education: Concepts and Practices.* San Francisco: Jossey-Bass, 1996.

ELAINE K. IKEDA is executive director of California Campus Compact and former project director of the University of California at Los Angeles Service-Learning Clearinghouse Project.

Index

Back Issue/Subscription Order Form

Copy or detach and send to:
Jossey-Bass Inc., 350 Sansome Street, San Francisco CA 94104-1342

Call or fax toll free!
Phone 888-378-2537 6AM–5PM PST; Fax 800-605-2665

Back issues: Please send me the following issues at $27 each.
(Important: Please include series initials and issue number, such as HE90.)

1. HE _____

_____

_____

$ _____ Total for single issues

$ _____ Shipping charges (for single issues *only;* subscriptions are exempt from shipping charges): Up to $30, add $5^{50} • $30^{01}–$50, add $6^{50} $50^{01}–$75, add $8 • $75^{01}–$100, add $10 • $100^{01}–$150, add $12 Over $150, call for shipping charge.

Subscriptions Please ❑ start ❑ renew my subscription to *New Directions for Higher Education* for the year _____ at the following rate:

U.S.	❑ Individual $59	❑ Institutional $114
Canada:	❑ Individual $59	❑ Institutional $154
All Others:	❑ Individual $83	❑ Institutional $188

$ _____ Total single issues and subscriptions (Add appropriate sales tax for your state for single issue orders. No sales tax on U.S. subscriptions. Canadian residents, add GST for subscriptions and single issues.)

❑ Payment enclosed (U.S. check or money order only)

❑ VISA, MC, AmEx, Discover Card # _____ Exp. date _____

Signature _____ Day phone _____

❑ Bill me (U.S. institutional orders only. Purchase order required.)

Purchase order # _____

Federal Tax ID 135593032   GST 89102-8052

Name _____

Address _____

_____

Phone _____ E-mail _____

For more information about Jossey-Bass, visit our Web site at:
www.josseybass.com   **PRIORITY CODE = ND1**

OTHER TITLES AVAILABLE IN THE
NEW DIRECTIONS FOR HIGHER EDUCATION SERIES
Martin Kramer, Editor-in-Chief

Printed in the United States
116072LV00002B/303/A

9 780787 957827